WHAT OTHERS SAY

CW00926531

A good overview on management and lea
guidance of everything needed to successfully navigate times of change. Making sense of Change Management remains essential reading for anyone who is currently part of, or leading, a change initiative. This book provides practical guidance you can immediately implement.

Olga Bird
Production Manager, Catherine Walker & Co

Change in any organisation is often met with feelings of apprehension which can result in defensive behaviour from employees. Cracking the Change Management Code addresses several key points such as the factors which cause such behaviours as well as solutions to them which begins with communication and implementing a "bottom -> up" approach.

The book also details the evolution of change management in the last 20 years displaying a clear understanding of how vital it is progress with the times, especially after the impact Covid-19 has had on organisations. Yvonne through her extensive research has learnt about the various human personalities and has demonstrated how change management techniques can be successfully applied to manage conflicts, or to motivate employees, leading to a significantly smooth transition/ completion for any project.

The book highlights the poignant impact Covid-19 has had on organisations and employees. The considerations which now need to be considered when hiring, training or even having workshops need to be thought of in a very different light. How do continue motivating the employee? How to keep a team synergy going? How to integrate a new employee so that they feel welcome, are all challenges which Cracking the Change Management code highlights and addresses.

Jilna Phillips
SAP S4 HANA Certified Finance Transformation Consultant

Having held a managerial position in the banking world for many years I see this book as a very useful guide for new change managers. It provides an excellent overview of change management, challenges that come with it and practical tips for resolution. Managing change in a larger organisation is a very challenging task and this book can absolutely ease the pain and make it smoother.

Anna Filatova
KYC/On-Boarding Manager, Goal Group of Companies

Cracking the Change Management Code is a useful book that focuses on the human aspect of change management, making the important assertion that is often neglected – that 'change is all about people and how best to manage them'. After all, an organisation's resources are their most important asset.

The book gives a brief history of Behavioural Change Management (BCM) before outlining effective strategies and best practices to manage people in helping the organisation achieve its objectives. Topics include an introduction to NLP, effective negotiation strategies, why good persuasion skills are essential in business change, how to overcome blockers to organisational change and manage conflict, plus how best to motivate in the workplace.

The book considers the impact of COVID-19 on organisational behaviour and what the change landscape may look like moving forward, before moving on to argue why all organisations cannot afford to neglect digital transformation, if they want to enhance their business' growth. The book is an enjoyable read and explores a multitude of very interesting topics.

Ian Jupp
Finance Partner at Lloyds Banking Group

Table of Contents

About this book

An organisation's best asset is its people. And change is about people. But if people are not prepared or able to make change, projects fail. Therefore to achieve desired outcomes, the people need to adopt the change.

In my experience, the only way to successfully deliver any change in an organisation is to crack the change management code: utilising the necessary change management methodologies and understanding human behaviour.

As the book demonstrates: with the right mindset and support, people of any level in a business have the power to both save projects from failure or deliver successful changes within their organisations. However, the entire change project team must be fully aligned and on board with the change, from the most junior to the highest senior leader... and the sponsor.

1. Why business change management is important

Post COVID-19 organisations worldwide have been forced to change their strategies and transform business models away from their traditional systems of how to serve their customers and towards a digital enhanced business model. This digital transformation has and will continue to change in the future, and employees will need to align to those changes, or they will be left behind.

Part of changing an organisation's business model includes considering its employees. However, changes to an organisation's business model do not mean the organisation is changing the behaviour of employees; it is the employees that adjust their behaviour towards the changes in the business model. Employees are the greatest asset to an organisation's strengths and weaknesses: they can enhance or disrupt an organisation.

1.1.   Causes of change

Organisational changes can be caused by internal or external factors. [1] The business initiates internal causes for organisational change. Examples include restructuring, expansion, contraction, management structure, and improvement in financial performance. External causes that require a business to change include government regulations, competitor intentions, technology, economic conditions, market conditions and consumer trends or attitudes.[1] The changes in the organisation can be incremental, by step or disruptive.

1.2.   What is behavioural change management?

Behavioural change management is defined as changing "the behaviour of the individual within the organisation".[2] However, behavioural change is not limited to an individual employee; it can be extended to a group of employees or all employees within an organisation.

Behavioural change has shifted significantly over recent years with the advent of the digital revolution and the COVID-19 pandemic. These two changes have seen organisations becoming increasingly virtual and their employees working remotely. Organisations quickly have to adapt to these changes in the real world to manage their workforce and survive.

1.3.   Three different types of change management

Changes within organisations are constant. They can be subtle or disruptive and occur at individual or team levels. These changes fit into three categories:[3]

1. DEVELOPMENTAL CHANGE occurs when an organisation recognises that there needs to be a change to improve an existing situation. This type of change is typically small, or the change can be in incremental improvements or corrections in the way an organisation conducts business.

2. TRANSITIONAL CHANGE occurs when an organisation needs to take a new direction because the existing direction is not working.[4]
3. TRANSFORMATIONAL CHANGE occurs when a new process creates itself due to the failure of another process.[4] This type of change is considered to be an overhaul and will include developmental and transitional changes.

Regardless of the type of change your organisation undergoes, the behavioural pattern of your employees will change. Some employees will accept change; others will reject and resist.

1.4.   The impact of not managing change

The organisational change serves to improve the operational and financial performance of the organisation.[5] Examples might include increasing revenue, reducing costs, improving cash flows or improving customer experience. The changes typically require amendments to the procedures or processes, and these changes can affect employee behaviour. Individuals or groups of employees may be reluctant to implement the changes, disrupting the organisation.

Disruption to organisational change needs to be avoided; therefore, it is crucial that the company leaders actively communicate with their employees. They must involve them in the organisational change and demonstrate how the changes will benefit the employees and the organisation. Failure to manage change through a lack of communication and involvement with employees will impact the organisation in many ways:[6]

- loss of improved operational and financial performance due to the change not being implemented efficiently by management and employees
- loss of the organisation's competitive advantage in the marketplace if the change is not implemented satisfactorily
- loss of key employees due to loss of morale or conflict within the organisation

- loss of employee morale due to the changes not suiting their ambitions
- employees may become resistant (actively or passively) to the organisation's change
- reduced employee productivity can occur at an individual or group level
- the workplace becomes disruptive
- small scale grievances can potentially escalate to large scale grievances.

NOTE: Smaller-scale grievances can often be far easier to resolve than large-scale ones.

1.5. Why change is difficult and the reasons for not liking change

Any change within an organisation can be difficult for an individual employee or group of employees to deal with;[7] therefore, the decision must be made as to whether an organisation change is necessary. Let's face it; organisational change is disruptive to any organisation, whether managed or not! The organisational change is challenging to implement for many reasons, including (i) loss of time, (ii) loss of productivity, (iii) additional training and (iv) the behavioural acceptance of the organisational change by the employees.

At the end of the day, the employees will decide (individually or collectively) whether or not they will adapt to change, and there are likely to be many reasons for their reluctance or resistance. Company leaders, directors, and management need to be aware of the specific resistance areas to help employees overcome their fear of change.

Let's take a look at some of the behavioural reasons why employees are resistant or reluctant to organisational change (Table 1):[6][7]

BEHAVIOURAL REASON	FACTORS
Fear of losing their job	• less working hours • working remotely • automation • new technologies
Reduced salary and benefits	• organisational change may result in reduced salary and benefits • less working hours resulting in loss of salary and benefits
Feeling overwhelmed or stressed	• overburdened with work • not enough time to consider the change • not feeling that the change will reduce their work burden • fear that the change will increase the workload, thus adding further pressure on being overburdened and stressed
Fear of Change	• departure from "the way it's always been done" • defensive behaviour to the new change • the change is not communicated well • comfortability with the present status quo • fear that the change will take them into unchartered territory • experience of previous organisational changes that have failed
Trust	• lack of trust that the change will bring forth the desired rewards

BEHAVIOURAL REASON	FACTORS
The change will deliver problems	• due to the unknown and limited factors about the impact of the change on the individual, we cannot always predict issues and how will everyone react and work with the changes • employees comfortable with the present status quo
Loss of power or authority	• fear applies to management as well as employees • management and employees dislike the loss of power and authority • employees can become more resistant to increased managerial control imposed upon them, particularly if they enjoy a high level of independence • demotion to a lower position
Transfer to another department	• employees or management may not have the necessary skills, experience or resources to perform their roles effectively
Dependence on other employees	• loss of support from other employees • change could threaten this dependence
Habits	• employees are settled with their existing habits • organisational change may require changes to habits that could meet resistance

BEHAVIOURAL REASON	FACTORS
Networking with other employees	• the COVID-19 pandemic is a classic example whereby the social networking structure with other employees was threatened when employees were forced to work from home • any new changes could disrupt the social networking structure
Resource availability	• change could limit the number of resources available for employees to perform their job roles effectively
Lack of information	• lack of information raises fear among employees about the impact of the change
Peer pressure	• peer pressure from other employees to accept or reject organisational change

Table 1: Reasons for behavioural resistance to change

1.6. Company leaders and management

Adopting behavioural change management within an organisation must start from the top leadership level. This can be the Board of Directors, company leaders or management. Managers cannot expect their employees to adopt changes if the managers are not willing to adopt the changes themselves. If managers are not aligned with the necessary changes, employees will notice this misalignment and feel concerned about the behavioural change.[7]

The decision to redesign and reshape behavioural change within an organisation must not be made by the Board of Directors, company leaders or management alone. Behavioural change should include the involvement and the listening of ideas from employees as they can contribute valuable ideas toward the reshaping of behavioural change. Gaining the contribution from employees serves many purposes, including:

- determining if the behavioural change is worthwhile and achievable
- employees feel more valued if they are listened to rather than just directed
- employees will be more adaptable to behavioural change if they are involved in reshaping it.

Communication of the behavioural change must flow from the top echelons of the organisation through to all employees. The purpose is to get the employees excited about the behavioural change and explain how their roles will impact the organisation's broader mission.[7] The employees' involvement during the process will minimise any negative aspects that could lead to a disruptive approach toward the behavioural change.

Chapter Summary

Organisations are constantly making changes to their business model. The recent COVID-19 pandemic has seen forced changes such as the way we work, automated systems and processes, and the move towards the digital world. These changes were needed for an organisation's business survival. Without forced changes, organisations would have faced closure which could have been permanent.

The implementation of change within an organisation needs to be carefully managed. If you want to implement change in your organisation successfully, you need to communicate the change to all employees and encourage them to be actively involved with the design and implementation of the change individually and collectively as a team.

No two people are the same. Everyone has different behavioural traits that impact their personal and work life. Some people will gladly accept change, while others will disrupt the change.

Adopting behavioural change management will progress the opportunity to achieve successful change within your organisation.

2. History of behavioural change management over the last 20 years

Behavioural change management has been studied as a topic since the early 19th century. Before this period, organisations did not necessarily consider the impact people could have on their operations. This chapter reviews the changes evident over the last two decades.

2.1. The movement of behavioural change management before 2000

Let's start with a brief overview of the development of behavioural change management before the last decade. Prosci mentions that Behavioural Change Management has gone through four periods: (i) Foundation (pre-1990), (ii) On the radar (the 1190s), (iii) Formalisation (the 2000s) and (iv) Going Forward.[8]

ORIGIN. The first era of behavioural change management began in 1909. Prosci calls this period the foundation era. Cultural anthropologist Arnold Van Gennep started studying the concept of change and recognised that there are three stages of change that can occur within people, namely (i) moving away from a current state through to (ii) transitioning and finally, (iii) changing into a future state.[8]

BEFORE 2000 (ON THE RADAR ERA). Behavioural change management became more predominant as other respected researchers and authors undertook studies on presenting theories, measuring and monitoring the impact of employees towards changes within organisations in the second era. Social psychologist Kurt Lewin presented a model known as the Three-Stage Model that uncovered how organisations could change the status quo for change.[8] The three stages were (i) unfreezing, (ii) transitioning to the change, and (iii) refreezing. More details about Lewin's model are explained in Chapter 8.

William Bridges, speaker and author, presented a similar three-stage model comprising of (i) the ending, (ii) entering the neutral zone, and (iii) moving into the new beginning.[8]

Abraham Maslow, the psychologist, developed a theory on human needs in 1943 and 1954. This theory was to help us understand our motivation for needs to be satisfied.[9] Human beings' needs range from simple to complex needs that must be constantly satisfied. Maslow identified the five types of needs that we are continually seeking as (i) psychological, (ii) safety, (iii) the sense of being loved and belonging, (iv) esteem and (v) self-actualisation. The first four needs are deficiency needs whilst the need for self-actualisation is a growth need.[10]

Other recognised researchers and authors who have shed their perspectives on behavioural change management include Kotter, LaMarsh and Johnson.

POST-2000. This period is known as the third era in behavioural change management (or the formalisation period mentioned by Prosci). It is when Behavioural Change Management began to form as a discipline, and more emphasis was placed on the psychological aspects, behaviour, and social impact of human behaviour.

The formalisation of the behavioural change management discipline was necessary if organisations wanted to achieve greater efficiencies and productivity through change. Managers and leaders had to come to grips with human behaviour and accept it can determine the success or failure of change within organisations. There needed to be a better understanding of individual human behaviour in the workplace, such as group dynamics, what causes conflicts, and employee motivation and expectations. Once leaders and managers have a broad concept of how individual human behaviour impacts change, they can devise solutions to deliver successful change.

Why do researchers need to understand individual human behaviour patterns? It is recognised that our behaviour will not change until a change occurs. We will continue with our daily routines as usual if there are no changes that confront us. The London School of Hygiene & Tropical Medicine describes our behaviour patterns as not changing when there is no external change, "like a train running along railway tracks".[11] In this example, our everyday routines are the same as a train running along a straight railway track with no deviations. However, if the train route differs by going on another track, individual behaviour changes until it gets used to the new route.

Prosci saw that the management process of behavioural change was to occur in three dimensions: (i) processes and tools, (ii) job roles and (iii) functions of an organisation.[8] His first dimension involved the development of tools, resources and processes based upon the prior foundations of behaviour change management. Managers and leaders could adopt these within their organisations. The second dimension mentioned by Prosci saw that organisations started to employ people who were solely responsible for change management in organisations. During this dimension, organisations began to develop the infrastructure to support change behaviour management. The third dimension gave rise to the adoption of the processes, resources and tools within organisations. Outside of organisations, the rise of professional associations took place in this third dimension.

2.2. Making behavioural change management sustainable

Today, behavioural change management has seen a shift towards more focus on sustainability and its impact on the world we live in.

Information technology & software

Technology has been a big winner in our personal and work life. An example provided by the London School of Hygiene & Tropical Medicine is the adoption of mobile phones in our daily life.[11] Mobile phones are consistently being updated with new features and have had a social impact on us: changing how we communicate in business and personally.

Nearly every organisation in the world uses technology or software: computers, servers, virtual networks, and software programs all help them operate their business model. Nowadays, they would find it highly challenging to manage without this information technology functionally. For example, video conferencing through software tools such as Skype, Zoom and Microsoft Teams proved popular during the COVID-19 pandemic.

Organisations worldwide have flourished by using technology and software to improve collaboration between managers and employees and increase communication between remote locations: gaining better insight into their business models. Leaders and managers have taken advantage of technology to improve outputs, automate manual systems, and improve operating efficiencies. Using technology to achieve the desired outcomes will ultimately place an organisation in a better financial position and possibly gain a better competitive advantage in the marketplace.

Continual training

Managers and employees must constantly undertake training for themselves and train their employees to maximise the opportunity to improve efficiency, productivity, and profitability. They will benefit from increasing their knowledge and learning new skills that can be used in the organisation.

Reinforcement learning

Reinforcement learning is typically associated with the training of machines such as computers to make a series of decisions.[12] However, reinforcement learning can also be applied to human behaviour and reward positive or unreward negative behaviour patterns. As human beings, we have different behavioural patterns that apply to our personal and work life. Sometimes our behavioural patterns need to be changed as individuals or teams within an organisation [11] if our old patterns do not fit with the culture, other employees, and the organisation's vision. Our behavioural patterns can be a block within a department or an organisation; therefore, they need to be reprogrammed to new patterns that balance with other team members, the culture, and vision.

Let us illustrate by example with the reinforcement learning of a personal behaviour pattern mentioned by Poddiachyi:[13] a baby learning to walk. The baby will learn by trial and error, trying to stand up and often falling, but persistence in standing up is the first positive step towards learning to walk. Once this step has been reinforced in the baby's mind, and with continued persistence, the baby will eventually take its first steps. The reward is often a big hug from the mother, and that reward becomes the motivation for the baby to continue with reinforced learning to walk.

This same type of example can be applied in the workforce by teaching employees or teams new behaviour patterns. For example, an organisation might undertake a change in accounting software. The new accounting software will require significant training upfront plus ongoing training. The learnings from the training must be reinforced to ensure that errors are minimised.

During this process, each person involved in the training will have a different behaviour pattern towards the change in the accounting software. Some employees will be receptive to the changes, while others will potentially be against the change, thus causing potential conflicts. This negative behavioural pattern can be disruptive to the department and the organisation. Reinforcement learning will be applied to those employees to improve their behaviour patterns so that the change to the new accounting software will be a success.

Sustainability

How do you make behavioural change management sustainable? The first step is to improve the technology and software within the company continually.

The second step is to enforce training and reinforced learning. Training and reinforced learning will reduce the possibility of errors and reward those people who succeed with positive behavioural change.

Behaviour Change Management is subject to a person changing their behaviour. However, the change must be sustainable and not a temporary change. People do not always make rational decisions as this depends upon their personality and emotions when making a decision. Decisions can be made automatically through unconscious processes or on the spur of the moment based on the available information.[14] However, the person may receive limited information and not make an effort to conduct due diligence on the matter and thus make a decision that is found to be irrational.

2.3.   Future outlook of behaviour change management

Prosci [8] identifies areas where Behaviour Change Management is likely to affect organisations in the future. These include:

1. The change capabilities of organisations will be developed and enhanced further. Organisations will embed change capabilities deeper into their organisation. The change capabilities will include changing the existing practices so that these practices will consider the human behaviour element. The change capabilities will address the competencies of managers and leaders. These capabilities will change to align with the organisation's values and statements.

2. Organisations will continue to invest in the latest change technology that will help with improving and monitoring change management. The technology can be equipment or software that will allow the leaders and managers to implement change management and enable them to monitor the effectiveness of new changes. There are two types of technologies that organisations can invest in: (i) tangible technology and (ii) intangible technology. Tangible change technology incorporates technology such as social media and technology used for digital transformation. Intangible change technology includes the expansion of neuroscience learnings (essential for understanding how the brain operates). Our brain is emotion-centric as it works on the experiences, thoughts, and sensations that produce emotional behaviour. Neuroscience has the potential to improve efficacy in the workplace.

3. There will be greater incorporation between PMOs and CMOs within organisations. This incorporation will happen at (i) the organisation level and (ii) the project level. There will be an increased level of collaboration between PMOs and CMOs at the organisation level, and both methodologies will likely be integrated. Project and change management will be integrated into one management at the project level. We will discuss PMOs and CMOs further in Chapter 12.

4. When leaders and managers have embraced behaviour change management as part of a normal process within a business, they will be required to continually undertake professional development in change management to advance their knowledge and skills within this field. This is similar to undertaking professional development in areas of speciality.

Chapter Summary

Behavioural Change Management has seen significant changes over the last two decades: organisations have more awareness and understanding of Behavioural Change Management. The discipline of Behavioural Change Management has been formalised through job roles (such as establishing change management offices), plus organisations have implemented their processes, systems, tools and resources to better control and manage human behaviour.

The future outlook for Behaviour Change Management sees growth within organisations. Accepting Behaviour Change Management will see leaders and managers undertake professional development. Organisations are likely to integrate PMOs and CMOs into one area at organisation and project levels. Existing practices will be modified and enhanced to include behavioural change. Organisations will continue to invest in future technology, but their investment will be targeted toward tangible and intangible change technology.

3. Change is about people and how best to manage them

For an organisation to move forward with its business model, the directors and management must have clear objectives in the short-mid to long term. There must be a roadmap identifying the milestones that need to be accomplished. The defined roadmap will take the organisation from its present position (position A) to the planned future position (position B).

To succeed in getting to position B requires the support and effort from your employees. The directors and management cannot do it alone; they need employees to assist them by working collectively as a team. Change within an organisation is about its people, but often, employees are aware that changes are implemented with or without communication.

In this chapter, the strategies and best practices are outlined on the best ways to manage people so that your organisation can achieve its objectives.

3.1. Why change is about people

It is important to consider that it is the people who change, not the organisation.[15]

> ## Organisations do not change.
> ## People change!
>
> *By Anita Baggio, Eleftheria Digentiki and Rahul Varma*
> *McKinsey and Company.*

There is a common misconception that organisations make the necessary changes to achieve their objectives. In reality, these changes are different financial or production targets, new technology, new supply chain directions, etc. These can easily be measured with key performance indicators. In some cases, the targets require a change in employee and management behaviour. The new targets are typically forced upon employees whilst forgetting about their behaviour towards change.

If an organisation does **NOT** achieve their proposed outcome, the blame is typically placed upon the management and employees' behaviour without examining the actual cause of the failure. There are many reasons why the organisation's outcomes were not achieved, such as technology, internal systems, market forces or economic conditions. Yet the failure to understand what has happened is a common problem in many organisations: it is too easy to place blame without further investigating the root cause.

The people, both managers and employees, are an organisation's best asset. The people can make the organisation successful or doomed as they are at the core of its activities from cleaning, administration, selling, marketing, IT and manufacturing.[16] Each person has a different behavioural pattern to work and their personal life; therefore, it is critical that their behaviour is understood so they can be managed; thus minimising the organisation's risk and setting the pathway forward to achieving the outcomes.

People dislike change unless they can see a personal benefit for themselves. They tend to resist the change and spend a minimal amount of time, effort and creative energy to help achieve the outcome of the change. For example, if a change reduces the workload on a person, they will enjoy and participate in this change. However, if the change results in an additional workload, there will be resistance, as it is not in the person's perceived interest, and they will see that their stress levels will increase.

Change management needs to be applied within an organisation to gain better control of people and begins with understanding each person's behavioural patterns, i.e., what drives them, what motivates them, etc.

When an organisation targets a change, there must be continued communication of that change from the leaders down to all employees. Leaders must clearly state the details, the reasons and the benefits that will accrue to the employees and the organisation. The communication must be tested to see if all employees clearly understand the messages.

Many organisations fail to communicate and test the communication. Consequently, this results in not knowing which employees support the change because they *want* to – or because they *have* to.

When a change is about to happen within an organisation, all employees should participate in setting the outcome of the change that will impact them directly… and indirectly. I state indirectly because personal behavioural bias can occur if they work on the change that impacts them directly. Hence, the reason for people to include the indirect impact as it will help other people within the organisation.

There are four benefits of a person being involved with the organisation's change. These benefits include:

1. People will become more inspired to accept the change rather than offer resistance.
2. They can take ownership of their change, thus giving them a sense of control.
3. They will become more committed to the change as they will not feel like the victim of change.
4. They will provide less resistance to the change.

> "Neuro-Linguistic Programming describes the fundamental dynamics between mind (neuro) and language (linguistic) and how their interplay affects our body and behaviour (programming)."
>
> *Robert B Dilts*

3.2.   What is NLP, and why use it in change management?

Neuro-Linguistic Programming (NLP) encompasses understanding the relevant components of human experience.[17] Dilts identifies the three most influential components that contribute to our human experience:

1. Neurology – regulates the functioning of our bodies.
2. Language – specifies how we interface and communicate with other people.
3. People – are programmed differently; therefore, we all behave differently.

NLP is a psychotherapy approach based upon a concept that reviews a person's behaviour regarding their thoughts, perception, and pattern of behaviour. This shapes the person into what they are today.[18] The concept relies upon a person's verbal, eye contact, and body language pattern, which are all forms of communication.[18] This concept requires understanding presuppositions that become the simple foundations of

NLP. There are 13 NLP presuppositions forming the foundations of NLP, and these presuppositions are quoted as listed in Table 2 below:[18]

NO.	NLP PRESUPPOSITION	EXPLANATION
1	If someone can do something, anyone can learn it	We all enjoy the capability of learning, and as such, we can learn anything if we adjust our mindset accordingly. Our behaviours will dictate to us whether to learn or not. Learning will lead to greater success. As global companies are transforming to a leaner digital business model, people will have to undertake new learnings if they still want to retain employment.
2	People already have all the resources that they need	It is commonly said that people can only perform their best with the available resources. These resources can be unlimited, but our state of mind can limit access to these resources. For example, if a person becomes overwhelmed, anxious or angry, these states will restrict them from accessing all available resources.
3	No person is considered to be wrong or broken. People will work to achieve the outcomes of what they are trying to accomplish	Each of us has ambitions and objectives that we wish to fulfil. Our objectives will focus on what is best for us. As such, we will work perfectly to accomplish these objectives. There is nothing wrong, and no one is wrong with this concept. However, understanding how that person functions will enable alternative solutions to be found to satisfy them and can achieve more usefulness.[19]

NO.	NLP PRESUPPOSITION	EXPLANATION
4	Failure is not acceptable, but there is feedback	Failures are not failures; they are life's important lessons. We should use failure as feedback. This feedback is an opportunity to learn from the mistakes so that a person can become stronger and better. The person can use the feedback to repeat the same task without the mistakes and become more efficient with the task.
5	You cannot fail to communicate	Communication is twofold: (a) verbal (talking or written) and (b) non-verbal (body language and eye contact). Every day, we express communication with our family, friends or work colleagues in some form.
6	Communication is more than what you are saying	Communication is not just about the words you speak; communication includes eye contact and body language.
7	The response that is obtained is the meaning of communication	The communication must be clear and specific. Failure to be clear and specific means you may get a different response from the receiver of the communication. [20] For example, you may ask your spouse for water. Your spouse may return with a bucket of water that is different from what you were expecting. The fault lies with not being specific in your communication.[20]

NO.	NLP PRESUPPOSITION	EXPLANATION
8	Try something different if you are not getting the response that you expect	If you keep performing the same tasks in the same manner, you will get the same result every time. You have to try different ways of performing the same tasks to get a different result.[20]
9	Every behaviour is useful in some context	Every behaviour has usefulness. The user may be wrong and does not serve the purpose of your organisation. It is important to understand the usefulness of the behaviour.
10	Behind every behaviour is a positive intention	A person's behaviour serves a purpose for them regardless of whether we consider that their behaviour is seen to be positive or negative. The person would intend that their behaviour aims to achieve something positive. If the positive intention can be found in a person's behaviour, then alternative behaviours can be found that can be used to suit the same purpose, which may not be harmful.[20]
11	Having a choice is better than not having any type of choice at all	Let's face it; if you are suffering a bad experience, it is much better to have a choice of solutions rather than no solution at all! You can assess which solution is best for you to overcome the bad experience. You will feel more positive, and the bad experience is no longer a problem. With no choice of solutions available, you are most likely to feel despondent, angry, sad or depressed.

NO.	NLP PRESUPPOSITION	EXPLANATION
12	The most influence is created when any system is flexible	Flexibility is a winner. Flexibility is the power to choose, thus giving a person more influence. A rigid system presents a barrier to flexibility.
13	The map is not the territory.	Our conscious awareness is limited. The way we perceive our values and beliefs will be different from other people, which is how we, as individuals, create our map.[20] We should respect the other person's map.

Table 2: NLP Presuppositions

Why is NLP used in change management? NLP is typically focused on changing individuals, teams and organisations to achieve a specific outcome. In simple terms, understanding a person's behaviour, how they think and how they react will enable organisations to think of alternate choices to overcome difficulties. The behavioural changes can be applied individually or collectively across teams or the organisation to achieve the objectives.

Most of us have heard about the Kotter Change Model. The Kotter Change Model is used to help diffuse employee resistance and reluctance to change within an organisation.[21] The model adopts a people-focused change structured approach in eight steps by focusing on creating a streamlined change process involving all key stakeholders. The NLP and the Kotter Change Model approaches can be used together to change the culture within the organisation and the behaviour of individuals and teams.

3.3.   How to negotiate for mutual benefit

3.3.1.   Why negotiation is important in change management

Negotiation is a process of compromise between two or more people to arrive at a better result for everyone. The negotiation process eliminates arguing and arrives at an agreement whereby all parties feel satisfied with the outcome.[22] Negotiation involves giving and taking by all parties and comprises three elements,[23] namely:

1. Two-way communication depends on the number of parties to arrive at a joint decision.
2. To find a mutually acceptable solution to the problem.
3. To achieve an amicable win-win solution for both parties.

Good negotiations can achieve business success and avoid future problems and conflicts. Negotiations will provide many benefits, such as helping you to build better relationships plus delivering quality solutions that will last a long time. Poor negotiations provide poor short-term solutions that do not satisfy the needs of either party. In many organisations, management and employees conduct negotiations with suppliers and customers. However, one of the most significant omissions within an organisation is the inadequate negotiation between management and employees. There may be subtle negotiations surrounding salaries and other resources, but there is a minor level of negotiation between management and employees when there is a change.

Change affects everyone within the organisation, from the directors to every employee, and equally impacts management and employees. Therefore, negotiation on changes needs to take place so that the chance of success is greater.

Let us look at some of the reasons behind the importance of negotiation in change management.

- Negotiations allow you to communicate concerns, needs and wants to reach a solid agreement and move forward in the climate of change.
- Key negotiation models are often not incorporated into change management, resulting in lost opportunities and dissatisfied stakeholders. Incorporating key change management principles is often neglected in the change management models, resulting in incomplete preparation and inadequate implementation.
- BATNA is an acronym that stands for Best Alternative to a Negotiated Agreement. It is defined as the most advantageous alternative the negotiating party can take if negotiations fail and an agreement is not found.[24] BATNA enhances your power in negotiation by mentioning that you have a stronger alternative solution in place. This negotiation power should motivate the other party to compromise.[25]

Win-win negotiation process

The Masterclass staff have identified five steps in the negotiation process that will arrive at a win-win outcome.[22] These five negotiation steps are shown in Figure 1.

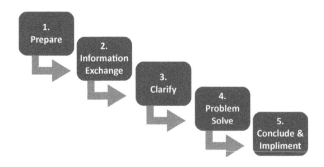

Figure 1: Negotiation Process

3.3.2. Learning the art of negotiation from the expert: Chris Voss

Chris Voss, a former FBI lead hostage negotiator, is a master of negotiation. He has spent more than 24 years of service with the Federal Bureau of

Investigation. During most of that time, he was the lead negotiator dealing with the most dangerous criminals across the globe. These criminals were involved with international kidnappings, and Chris was responsible for safely securing the release of these hostages.

He has gained many effective negotiation strategies and skills during his service with the FBI and later in the private sector and government. His strategies are designed to resolve conflicts and conclude with successful business negotiations.

Mr Voss has outlined his own 7 Principles of Negotiation.[26] Let's take a moment to understand his process for successful negotiation. We can learn from these principles to apply in our businesses:

1. Begin with an accusations audit.
2. It is in the best interest to use active listening to examine the motivational factors of the other side.
3. Apply empathy with the other side.
4. Examine the other side's speaking patterns.
5. Observe the body language of the other side.
6. Keep the other side away from speaking with dishonesty.
7. The win-win situation is the preferred outcome.

3.3.3. Undue influence in negotiations

The negotiation process's desired outcome is to arrive at a win-win position for all parties involved – and many theories have been put forth regarding how to arrive at that win-win outcome.

For example, all parties involved in the negotiation process must be given equal opportunity to participate in the process. Hayes states that undue influence occurs *"when an individual can persuade another's decisions due to the relationship between the two parties."*[27] Management is a prime candidate for applying undue influence on their employees as they are in a position of power. The undue influence applied to employees will typically not be in their long-term best interest, and the employees become less motivated and cooperative. The rift between management and employees widens, thus potentially causing more disruption towards change.

If one party applies more influence than any other party, they would be exerting undue influence on all other parties; therefore, the negotiation process becomes worthless.

3.4. How to manage difficult people

3.4.1. What is a difficult person?

Typically, one employee in most organisations can be classified as a difficult person! Difficult people can be found across all industry sectors and any size organisation. However, there is an underlying problem if you have more than one difficult person in your organisation. The problem may not be related to the employee(s) but the organisation's culture. The organisation's culture would need to be fixed as a priority before any management of behavioural changes can be applied.

Is there a secret way to manage difficult people? First, we must define what a difficult person in the workplace is. Let's look at a few of the types of traits that classify (but are not limited to) a difficult person:[28]

- a person who stays up to date with the office gossip
- the quiet employee who appears to be distant or withdrawn
- an employee who is stressed out
- an employee who has to be in control and is known as the "Control Freak"
- an employee who is paranoid
- an employee who never accepts responsibility or admits to their errors. These employees are known as blame shifters
- an arrogant employee
- a backstabbing employee who enjoys telling on a colleague or takes credit for work they have not undertaken.

If you have an employee who fits into one of the categories listed above, you will need to deal with them before the rot spreads throughout your organisation. Dealing with difficult people is not easy and can be challenging depending on the type of difficult person and the situation you face. You may know of the "rotten apple" idiom whereby:

> **"A bad or corrupt person in a group, typically one whose behaviour is likely to have a detrimental influence on their associates."**
>
> *Oxford Dictionary*

A "rotten apple" employee can cause much disruption throughout your organisation, similar to a computer virus spreading through your computer network. This type of employee is disruptive and causes chaos throughout an organisation.

3.4.2. Solutions available for managing difficult people

Many solutions can be applied to managing difficult people in your organisation and do work, depending upon how ingrained the traits are within the person.

Table 3 highlights some of the solutions you can implement in your organisation:[28][29][30]

TRAIT	SOLUTION
Gossip	• do not give out information that can be spread around the organisation • stay clear of the employee
Quiet employee	• be friendly • give them space to open up
Stressed out employee	• don't overwhelm them • break down the work into manageable steps
Control Freak	• give them clear, detailed reports and updates on projects • avoid ambiguity, so they do not want to gain greater control • do not give them attention
Paranoid employee	• be careful with the words spoken • keep employees up to date with what's happening in the office to reassure them nothing is being kept from them
Blame shifters	• discuss the details of the project • determine responsibilities • determine deliverables required
Arrogant employee	• praise them when they deserve praise • offer positive feedback before criticism
Backstabbing employee	• confront issues with them face to face

Table 3: Solutions to managing difficult employees

A conflict often occurs when someone criticises the person; therefore, it is crucial to avoid confrontation when dealing with difficult employees. [30] The most suitable solution to avoiding confrontation is to criticise the behaviour and not the employee.

3.5. How to deal with different types of personalities and people

An organisation is filled with many types of employees based upon gender, age, religion, skills and experience. Each employee has an individual personality that will differ from other employees. There are seven key personality traits that you should be aware of that will exist in your organisation, according to Codella and Wyles. Codella is a Senior Content Marketing Manager for Wrike. Wyles is the managing director of Festo Training.[31][32]

PERSONALITY TRAIT	WARNING SIGNS	CHANGE MANAGEMENT STEPS
The Sceptic	• the state that everything is fine • there is no way to gain better results • they make opinions before trying the change	• give them responsibility • encourage their feedback with ideas
Eager Beaver	• enthusiastic, eager and impulsive employee	• use their enthusiasm to get other employees pumped up • map out a road to success

PERSONALITY TRAIT	WARNING SIGNS	CHANGE MANAGEMENT STEPS
Free spirit	• they are hesitant to follow processes and do not like unnecessary documents • do not follow convention	• give them autonomy so that they can enjoy their freedom • do not restrict or confine them
Champion	• fully engaged and aligned with the organisation • enjoy the immense drive • pro-active	• offer them more projects, with each project being more difficult than the previous project • praise them for their efforts
Ambassador	• fully engaged and aligned with the organisation • enjoy the immense drive	• encourage them to be more pro-active • promote them to a champion when the timing is right
Challenger	• essential player if given all of the information • not as pro-active	• support them with positive feedback • increase their motivation level
Saboteur	• a person who likes to cause disruption • not satisfied with their role	• switch their role to another area where they will be satisfied, providing they have the skills and experience

Table 4: Personality traits to watch out for

Chapter Summary

An organisation's best asset is its people. And change is about people. Therefore to achieve their desired outcomes, they (the people) will need to adopt the change. Those people will accept or resist change depending upon their behavioural traits. Every person has different behavioural traits: some of these traits may be good, while others may be negative. The negative traits can be individualised or quickly spread throughout the organisation and significantly impact achieving the desired outcomes.

This chapter has covered the essential elements of managing difficult people and discovering the early warning signs to watch out for based on an individual's personality.

4. Why good persuasion is needed in business change

Organisational change is disruptive to any organisation regardless of the change being managed properly. Let's revisit an earlier section of this book where I discussed that organisational change is often difficult for employees. I explained that employees will decide whether or not they will adapt to change and that decision will be made individually or collectively by the group or all employees. There are many reasons why employees are reluctant or resistant to organisational change.[33]

The art of persuasion is used for both positive and negative behaviour in business and in our personal lives. In business, persuasion can be used to intentionally change its employees' behavioural patterns, attitudes, or beliefs so that the organisation can successfully achieve its objectives – it can be a powerful tool!

Persuasion is designed to encourage employees to follow a particular course of action intentionally. Therefore, leaders and managers need to have the skill of persuasion.[34] They must be able to convince their employees that a particular change is essential for the organisation. For example, the leaders and managers may request that all employees wear a uniform during working hours or when visiting clients. Employees may resist this change, and if they do, it is the responsibility of the managers and leaders to persuade the employees that this change is needed and will be for their benefit.

Persuasion can also be used in the opposite manner, as employees can use the art of persuasiveness with their leaders. For example, an employee might have discovered a more suitable way to eliminate a manual process by introducing new technology, improving efficiency and reducing operating costs. The employee would need to convince the leader to introduce the new technology through persuasion.

This chapter illustrates certain strategies and techniques of persuasion that you can introduce into your organisation today. Consider adopting persuasion techniques and strategies such as being an active listener, understanding body language, using emotional intelligence, applying logic and reasoning when communicating, and describing the benefits to the employees. Using these powerful techniques and strategies will influence and benefit your employees so that your organisation can implement the planned changes for future success.

4.1. Being a good listener

Communication involves the art of listening and speaking to other people; however, there are many shortfalls to the skill of successful communication. In this segment, the art of listening is explored.

Do you *really* listen to what other people are saying? Many people confuse listening with hearing. Matt Toledo, a member of the Forbes Los Angeles Business Council, reports that hearing occurs when a person is only partially engaged in the conversation because they have an agenda they wish to push onto the other person(s).[35] Hearing does not involve effort, and there is no intention to actively engage in the conversation, according to Dom Barnard, co-founder of VirtualSpeech.[36] Dom is a regular contributor to VirtualSpeech (a business specialising in world-class soft skills training and development programs for teams within organisations).

Listening is a master skill in communication that most of us can improve upon as it involves "identifying the sounds of speech and processing them into words and sentences".[37] It requires concentration and focuses upon the other person communicating – often referred to as active listening. Better listening skills can only be achieved through practice.

Active listening requires a person to devote their full attention to the other person to understand the other person before they offer their response. It shows that you are fully engaged and interested in what the other person says to you. There is an intention to be actively involved to find a win-win situation for the other person and yourself [36]. Active listening consists in understanding the other person, empathising with their situation and building trust with the other person. This concept will make finding a solution to conflicts and resistance easier.

Active listening comes in the form of verbal and non-verbal communication. The following table contains some common signs of both:[36]

VERBAL COMMUNICATION	NON-VERBAL COMMUNICATION
• Remembering key information or point of the conversation • Reinforcement of the person's conversation to ensure clarity of the situation • Questioning	• Eye contact with the other person • Smile with the other person • Posture will determine the other person's intent of listening or hearing • Not distracted by other sounds or events

Table 5: Verbal and Non-verbal Communication Signs

In the workplace, active listening is an essential interpersonal skill and applies to all people, from the top segment to the bottom segment of the organisation. As a leader or manager, this interpersonal skill will help you understand your team and manage and delegate workflow.[38] The most critical steps of active listening are to be able to (a) ask questions and (b) repeat what the other person has mentioned: ensuring that you have a clear understanding of the other person's comments.[35]

Active listening is also an important step toward defusing challenges in the workplace and offers the opportunity to find solutions to the challenge.

Active listening in the workplace offers nine benefits:[39][38]

1. The ability to connect more easily with all types of people and their behaviours.
2. The ability to increase your capacity to retain more information which serves for better clarity of any situation.
3. The ability to build more knowledge which will help resolve conflict.
4. The ability to build relationships.
5. The ability to build trust.
6. The ability to identify and anticipate problems to avoid nasty surprises happening later.
7. The ability to create an easier pathway to resolve conflict.

8. The ability to empower you as a leader or authoritarian.
9. The ability to set priorities more easily.

Each of the nine benefits of active listening listed will enable leaders to resolve conflicts by understanding the other person's behaviour.

Catherine Moore has over 20 years of experience working for the non-profit sector as a certified change expert. Moore is a member of the Association of Change Management Professionals (ACMP) in Canada and has written an article for Heller Consulting. She points out that a high level of change initiatives do not succeed due to a lack of strong leadership. [40] She mentions that the chances of successful change initiatives are greater with strong leadership. Strong leadership requires deep listening. The perspective of active listening applies to individual people within an organisation and departments. Each group (department or team) will have a different perspective on the change initiative. However, deep listening should not only be limited to when change occurs. Deep listening should be built into the organisation's culture, and every person should participate.

Therefore, being a good listener will enable that listener to identify challenges and prevent them from occurring or reduce the risk of the challenge spreading throughout the organisation.

4.2.   Body language

Body language lays the foundation for a deeper level of communication than verbal communication. Information can be conveyed through nonverbal communication and verbal communication.[41] It is a powerful form of nonverbal communication that most of us express and interpret in different ways. There are three aspects of body language – (i) eye contact, (ii) personal space and (iii) posture.[42]

Management must identify the nonverbal cues (physical behaviour, expressions, and mannerisms) or signs as this will allow them to judge the reaction based on their communication. Nonverbal cues and signs can differ significantly depending upon how the communicator delivers the message.

Albert Mehrabian (a body language expert and Professor of Psychology at UCLA) developed his model on the elements of a face-to-face conversation. His study found that effective communication was supported by 55% body language, 38% tone of voice and 7% related to words.[43] It can be seen that the body language and tone of voice used were more important than the words.

So if we use the previous example of staff uniforms to illustrate: a manager states that all employees must wear uniforms in a demanding voice. Some employees will agree whilst other employees will resist. The way that the message is delivered, in this case, in a demanding manner, will likely see more resistance from employees. The manager will be able to observe the reaction through the body language given by the employees – likely to be negative body language. If the delivery of the message to the employees were less demanding, there would be a greater chance of receiving positive body language from employees meaning more acceptance of the message.

Different reactions can occur between verbal and nonverbal communication. In the requirement to wear uniforms example, some employees may verbally agree to the change, but their body language may differ, giving a mixed message.

How do you differentiate between positive and negative body language cues? Here are some points of differentiation (Table 6) between positive and negative body language cues.[44][41]

POSITIVE BODY LANGUAGE CUES	NEGATIVE BODY LANGUAGE CUES
• upright posture • maintain good eye contact • nodding your head • offering a firm handshake • leaning in towards the communicator whilst listening • minimal facial expressions • smiling • raising eyebrows • open palms • repetitive actions • pointing to a subject whilst talking	• folding your arms across the body • multiple facial expressions • slouched posture • not maintaining good eye contact • the handshake is limp • biting lips • head in hands • hands on hips • fidgeting • finger tapping • crossing the legs away from the communicator

Table 6: Body language cues

4.3. Emotional intelligence

Emotional intelligence can be used throughout an organisation by leaders, managers and employees. Emotional intelligence aims to understand a person's emotions so that their emotions can be expressed and managed. Kendra Cherry, a psychology education consultant, has cited the definition of emotional intelligence as set out by psychologists Peter Salovey and John D. Mayer as "the ability to recognize and understand emotions in oneself and others".[45]

Daniel Goleman, psychologist, science journalist and author, has published his emotional intelligence theory. This theory consists of five elements, as illustrated in Figure 2.[46]

Figure 2: Five elements of emotional intelligence theory

Emotional intelligence can be used to great advantage by understanding a person's emotions so that these emotions can be managed to make sound decisions and make changes. Emotional intelligence can be used in the workplace effectively to (i) achieve a shared vision, (ii) motivate other members, (iii) improve communication and (iv) make changes within the organisation.

Cathy Cassata, health, mental health and medical news writer, outlines the benefits of an organisation applying emotional intelligence in the workplace.[47] The benefits include:

- teamwork
- encouraging employees to be engaged
- building essential social skills
- building stronger leaders
- motivated employees.

4.4. Explain the logic, reasoning and benefits to the employees

Logic is the study of arguments that have been presented systematically. What is reasoning? Reasoning is the application of making sense of events and circumstances surrounding us using the logic technique. The use of logical sense provides better clarity of the circumstances or events, enabling better judgment. In the workplace, it is crucial to explain to the person they need to change their behaviour or adapt to the change using the techniques of logic and reasoning.[48]

For example, if a leader or manager simply tells a person to make a change without any logic or reasoning supporting the change, the leader or manager is likely to be faced with resistance from that person. Therefore, the manager or leader must explain the logic behind the change. Explaining the reasons to the person provides a greater chance of that person accepting the change. It is important to support the reasons with evidence to build a powerful and convincing argument. Armed with all of the information and facts, the person will understand the logic and the reasoning behind the change, allowing that person to commit to the change.

Every person has a different perspective in life which provides different behavioural patterns. One such behavioural pattern is emotion. We all have feelings, but these feelings will differ from each other. A person's emotions can get out of control, thus preventing that person from functioning and thinking properly. Many techniques are available to help manage a person's emotional level. It has been suggested that logical reasoning can be employed to manage these emotions.[49]

Part of the persuasion tactics that should be used is explaining to employees the benefits attached to the change.[44] If the employee can see that the benefits will offer advantages to them personally, they will most likely accept the change. If the change does not result in personal advantages for the employee, the employee will most likely resist the change.

4.5. Establishing credibility

What is meant by the term 'credibility'? This term is defined as a person or organisation that "can be believed or trusted".[50] Marcus Lemonis, a successful entrepreneur and advocate, further clarifies the term credible. Marcus, who has helped many struggling businesses on CNBC's The Profit Show, states that a person or organisation is deemed to be credible if they are seen to have the qualities of being reliable and their communications are plausible.[51]

To encourage others to accept you, you must establish your credibility by developing strong, positive, sincere and sustainable relationships with them. Remember that it takes time to become credible (whether you are a manager or an employee), as you need to build trust, be a source of information and have the ability to make decisions. If you fail to deliver on your promise, you become less credible.

Being recognised as a credible person will enable you to use your persuasion skills to alter people's behavioural patterns. People's behavioural patterns are likely to change if they are persuaded by a credible authority within the organisation. The authority would be seen as a person who can be believed and trusted, and people make faster decisions if they can rely upon a credible person.

Once credibility has been employed throughout all levels of people within your business, your organisation will be deemed credible by its stakeholders (investors, banking institutions, taxation authorities, customers and suppliers). Lemonis points out that an organisation may offer the greatest product or service, but it will suffer accordingly if the organisation and its people are deemed not to be credible.[51]

4.6. Being honest and sincere with employees

Leaders should recognise the importance of communicating the positive and negative aspects of a person's role or a change within an organisation. [52] Honesty applies in two forms. The first form is that leaders should be forthcoming with the truth to their employees. The second form is that employees should be honest with their leaders by having the ability to voice their opinions. When voicing their opinions, employees are responsible for backing them up with facts in the same manner as leaders.[52] There should be no reprisal system in the organisation that will prevent employees from candidly being able to express their opinions. Leaders should be able to accept their employee's assessments without making a personal judgement,[52] and leaders should be objective with their evaluations.

Despite the outcome of the recognition for performance/underperformance or acceptance/resistance, being honest and sincere with an employee will enable them to understand their circumstance fully. The employee should then understand and appreciate the honesty, move forward positively, and improve their performance or accept the change within the organisation.

Most people in the workplace are seeking one longing. They want to be recognised as important [71] and want to be appreciated for their efforts. If an employee is performing well, congratulate them and thank them for their efforts. If an employee is underperforming, discover the issues for the underperformance and motivate the employee to perform better. There may be various reasons the employee is underperforming, such as behavioural, attitude, belief, or inadequate skills. This underperformance may require additional training to change the actions to produce a better performance.

Consideration of the employee and their feelings during change are paramount as certain factors could make them feel frustrated or disappointed. There are two options for the employee. They will either express their opinion (and that opinion can be positive or negative), or they will not say anything. Not being honest with an employee may deepen their frustration or inner disappointment, and leaders should be aware that honesty can cause disruptions, such as increased resistance to change.

The organisation's culture should foster an honesty system with every person: it will result in a more positive attitude, and acceptance of change becomes more realistic.

4.7. Persuasion through the 'Herd Effect'

You will find in many organisations that some employees look up to other employees to see their behavioural patterns or decisions before making their own. This is commonly referred to as the 'herd effect'.[44] The 'herd effect' impact can be used quite effectively as a persuasion tactic for changing an employee's behaviour or resistance to the organisation's change. Management can use the 'herd effect' positively to persuade and demonstrate to resistant employees that other employees or other organisations have adopted the change.

Examples:

1. The finance department will transfer a new accounting software to a modern software package. Nine out of ten employees in the finance department accept the decision to change, so the tenth employee will combine with the other nine employees and accept the change. The 'herd impact' results in a positive impact on the organisation.

2. The management has decided not to distribute the end of year bonus to employees due to the financial impact of the COVID-19 pandemic. Four out of five employees in the organisation have resisted this change. Consequently, the fifth employee makes the same decision as the other employees ('Herd Effect'), i.e., to follow the other employees by resisting the change. All employees have reacted negatively to the proposed change.

Chapter Summary

Changing within an organisation is disruptive in itself without incurring disruption from employees who are resistant to the change.

Persuasion is a powerful tool, and all organisations should adopt this tool to improve efficiencies and make changes. This tool should be used to convince employees about the need for change within your organisation. Persuasion is intentionally designed to encourage employees to follow a particular course of action. It can also be used to temper negative beliefs, attitudes or behavioural patterns within an individual or group of employees.

This chapter has listed several techniques: active listening, body language, establishing credibility, and emotional intelligence to ensure honesty and sincerity. All can be employed throughout all levels of your organisation today. Applying these persuasion techniques will give your next business change an improved chance of success without being burdened with the loss of time, inefficiencies, and additional costs.

5. How to best motivate in the workplace

Organisations that instil a culture of accountability and transparency will find that they will enjoy better performance, productivity and profitability. This type of culture will allow the organisation to become more flexible, more competitive in the market, and more responsive to customer needs. To achieve this, the organisation needs motivated employees.

Motivation is a key strategy that can be used in the workplace to encourage individuals and groups of employees to perform better, improve efficiencies and make change happen. Throughout this chapter, I explain how you can use motivation to encourage individuals and teams to adopt change.

Psychology education expert Kendra Cherry states that motivation is a process that makes a person act to achieve what they desire.[53] A team of motivated employees is visible to your external stakeholders. It will also help you achieve a competitive advantage as motivated employees will have higher productivity levels, so the cost of labour will be reduced. Conversely, a demotivated team of employees can destroy relationships with external stakeholders, and you will likely lose your competitive advantage.

What behavioural patterns make a person motivated to achieve their desire? Cherry states that motivation is the driving force behind a person's action. The "biological, emotional, social, and cognitive forces" drive the behavioural patterns.

Motivation is one of the success factors that should be applied within an organisation, according to authors Professor Buchanan and Dr Huczynski. The two authors look at the impact of organisational behaviour from a team and individual employee perspective (Buchanan, Prof. D. & Huczynski, Dr A., 2020). Let's explore some simple techniques such as goal setting and utilising the social process of influencing others to give you better guidance on how you can apply motivation to any type of person or group regardless of their personality type and traits.

5.1.   The organisation must have values

Respected authors Ken Blanchard and Norman Vincent Peale examined the profitability levels of the top 500 organisations over many years. They found that within those 500, the top 20% in each industry sector had achieved higher profits over many years because their (written) values were instilled throughout the organisations. All people within these organisations lived by and breathed these values every day. Organisations with values and who are committed to quality are likely to attract and retain high-calibre people. If the high-calibre people are surrounded by like-minded people, they will tend to work harder to become higher-performing people.

The organisations that fell within the 80% bracket did not achieve consistently high levels of profitability over the many years of the study. The authors noted that some of these organisations had put values in place, but they were not instilled in everyone; therefore, few people knew of them or practised them. You cannot embrace something you are unaware of!

Einstein's famous quote of *"nothing happens until something moves"* can be applied here: nothing will happen in the organisation until someone takes action to improve performance. The present and future quality managers and leaders are those capable of extracting high performance from ordinary people. Motivation is a key strategy that can be used in the workplace to increase performance and enact change.

5.2.   Types of motivation

Although there are many, it is generally accepted that there are two *main* types of motivation – (i) intrinsic and (ii) extrinsic.[54] The intrinsic and extrinsic types of motivation are recognised in the incentive theory of motivation. Intrinsic motivation occurs when a person decides to achieve an action based on their internal desire. For example, a person may wish to quit smoking. The desire to quit smoking is caused by the inner feeling of wanting to improve their health. Extrinsic motivation occurs when a person is motivated to achieve an action based upon external forces influencing their behaviour. Using the same example about smoking, a doctor may advise the person to quit smoking. The doctor is the external force motivating the person to quit smoking.

The same types (intrinsic and extrinsic) of motivation apply in the workplace. An intrinsic example is an employee seeking promotion. An employee rewarded with a bonus based on personal performance would be an extrinsic motivator. The employee wants to improve their performance to receive a bonus; therefore, in this example, both intrinsic and extrinsic motivators come into play with the employee wanting to improve their performance so that they can be rewarded with a promotion (intrinsic) and a bonus (extrinsic).

Managers can encourage motivation within the organisation through contact with the employees. Positive contact will foster higher performance levels through higher productivity and profitability. The present and future performance of the organisation is determined when there is positive contact between the manager and the employee. The opposite scenario occurs when there is negative contact between the manager and the employee. The employee will fear rejection and failure and will only complete the work needed to be completed and no more. The organisation's performance will suffer through lower productivity and profitability. The key point raised is that managers need to be good at extracting peak performance from each employee to maximise the organisation's performance.

Managers can encourage motivation within the organisation through contact with the employees. Positive contact will foster higher performance levels through higher productivity and profitability. The present and future performance of the organisation is determined when there is positive contact between the manager and the employee. The opposite scenario occurs when there is negative contact between the manager and the employee, as the employee will fear rejection and failure. The employee will only complete the work that is needed to be completed. The organisation's performance will suffer through lower productivity and profitability. The key point raised is that managers need to be good at extracting peak performance from each employee to maximise the organisation's performance.

5.3. How to motivate individuals and teams

5.3.1. Theories of motivation

There have been many motivation theories that accredited researchers have put forth; most of these theories have limitations.[55] The most common motivation theories are shown in Table 7.[55][56]

MOTIVATION THEORY TITLE	BRIEF POINTS ABOUT THE THEORY
Incentive Theory	<ul><li>applies to teams and individuals</li><li>intrinsic and extrinsic</li><li>the reward is the motivator to take action</li><li>the higher the reward, the greater the motivation to take action</li></ul>
Instinct Theory	<ul><li>the motivation for behaviour is based upon their internal evolutionary programming</li><li>this internal evolutionary programming becomes human instinct for basic survival</li><li>survival instincts include fear, anger, love, shame, and modesty</li></ul>
Drive Theory	<ul><li>this theory suggests that people are driven to meet their unmet needs and will thus be motivated to take action</li></ul>
Arousal Theory	<ul><li>this motivational theory works around the person's feeling of arousal.</li><li>high arousal suggests action to lower the feeling of arousal</li><li>low arousal suggests action to increase arousal feeling</li></ul>

MOTIVATION THEORY TITLE	BRIEF POINTS ABOUT THE THEORY
Maslow's Hierarchy of Needs Theory	• two components: (i) societal class and (ii) human needs • top hierarchy – self-actualisation • second hierarchy – esteem • third hierarchy – love and belonging • fourth hierarchy – job security (safety) • fifth hierarchy (bottom) – motivated to satisfy basic (psychological) needs

Table 7: Theories of Motivation

5.4.2. Importance of goal setting

The leaders and managers of organisations will (usually) have grand goals that they want to achieve, but how will they motivate individual employees and teams not just once but continually to accept and strive to achieve them?

Firstly, the grand goals must be achievable and SMART. [57]

S	SPECIFIC	the goals must be simple and sensible
M	MEASURABLE	the goals must be capable of being measured
A	ACHIEVABLE	the goals must be attainable
R	RELEVANT	the goals must be realistic and relevant to what the organisation is trying to achieve
T	TIME-BOUND	The goals cannot be endless; they must have a definite end time

Table 8: SMART goals

Secondly, the grand goals must be broken into smaller goals (sub-goals). The smaller goals must be aligned to the grand goals and follow the principle of being SMART. These sub-goals will be divided among teams and individual employees.

Thirdly, the sub-goals must be measurable using tools like Key Performance Indicators (KPI) and Key Performance Ratios (KPR). The measurement of the sub-goals will give clear guidance as to the achievement of the organisation's grand goals.

5.3.3. Behaviour

Motivating employees is challenging, but it is important to understand what motivates employees to perform a behaviour. For example, there are many reasons why people get out of bed every day: school, work, exercise, taking care of children, shopping and so forth. Each of the reasons mentioned is driven by different motives to perform the behaviour.

Three factors play into a person's motivation to participate in a behaviour:[2]

1. The person's positive or negative attitude toward the behaviour. The attitude considers if the outcome of the behaviour is positive and worth the effort of the behaviour.
2. The subjective norms associated with that behaviour based upon other people's perception and approval/disapproval of that behaviour.
3. Competence to complete the behaviour. Does the person have the capability, competence, and confidence to complete the behaviour? If not, there has to be an understanding of barriers or obstacles that prevent the person from completing the behaviour.

Behaviour can be influenced and managed if a person's motives can be understood.

Psychological factor

Highly acclaimed personal development expert, Mr Brian Tracy, states that if an organisation wants to gain better productivity and performance, it must use the psychological factor to motivate individuals and teams of employees. Because it demonstrates why companies succeed and fail, the psychological factor has been one of the strongest breakthroughs in management in recent decades, showing that:

- across all industries, 20% of the organisations will generate 80% of the overall industry profits
- the most talented people are attracted to these organisations and why)
- people working in the top organisations will outperform those same type of people working in average or below-average organisations.

The psychological factor harnesses the motivators and power to achieve better productivity and performance. The psychological factor has not been used widely. This explains why some organisations have not been able to harness their people's capability, enthusiasm, commitment, and energy to seek better results.

As a manager or leader, you can apply this psychological factor within your organisation. Try applying the psychological factor to yourself first, then apply it to other employees; it can improve motivation to better performance, productivity, and quicker results.

Employees love to be motivated to higher levels as this improves their self-concept. What do we mean by self-concept? Self-concept is recognised as a person's values, attitudes, opinions and belief structure. In simple terms, self-concept is understanding how a person sees themselves, how they feel and what they believe.

From early childhood to the present day, self-concept governs our performance behaviour based on our personality and will differ between all people. The output of our self-concept will vary in respect to improvements in performance.

Carl Rogers, a humanist psychologist, states three components of self-concept:[58]

1. **SELF-IDEAL.** This component focuses on what the individual wants from life now and in the future that can be potentially gained from their dreams, hopes, goals and aspirations. The self-ideals can be influenced by their [personal] desires and their desires in the workplace. Their workplace desires can be influenced by the organisation's values, culture, governance and role models.

2. **SELF-IMAGE.** This component looks at how a person feels about themselves. Their self-image is greatly influenced by how other people perceive them and how they are treated. These perceptions will result in a positive or negative self-image of themselves. A person with a positive self-image has resulted from other people giving that person respect, positive feedback, love and a level of importance. A person who possesses such a positive image will be a high performer and requires less motivation. A person with a negative self-image lacks the enthusiasm to be a high performer due to receiving negative feedback. From others' perception, they believe they have no importance and do not deserve respect.

3. **SELF-ESTEEM.** This component reviews how a person values themselves based on their role in society and how others perceive them. People that enjoy high self-esteem set themselves higher standards and higher performance levels. The two factors of higher standards and higher performance levels can positively and negatively impact your organisation. The positive impact of self-esteem is that it can flow through to all other people within the organisation and drive higher standards and performance. However, the negative impact is that it can also disrupt as not everyone in an organisation might be *able* to achieve higher standards and performance.

Leaders and managers need to develop an environment of high self-esteem. This environment can be developed by removing the fear of failure and rejection that inhibits personal performance. A high self-esteem environment will foster lower employee turnover, absenteeism and productivity.

People in the workplace are seeking two fundamental needs to boost their self-esteem – (i) autonomy (recognition) and (ii) dependency (acceptance). People thrive upon being autonomous as it allows them to demonstrate their performance and be recognised for their performance. People seek dependency to feel accepted and that the organisation relies upon their performance to achieve the goals. The person wants to feel that they are part of the team within the organisation. Therefore, managers and leaders can foster a positive environment by promoting autonomy for individuals whilst accepting them as part of the organisation's team.

Using key performance indicators

An organisation can analyse its success in achieving its goals by using key performance indicators (KPIs).[59] There are two types of KPIs – (i) high-level, focusing on the complete organisation and (ii) low-level, concentrating on a specific area of the organisation, such as the sales or marketing department.

The most popular and relevant KPIs link to Employee Engagement. If the KPIs are chosen and implemented well, employees will feel more motivated and have greater control over their performance, leading to the organisation's growth.

Employee Engagement needs to be measured as (i) it influences the organisation's objectives, (ii) it raises the bar for increased employee loyalty and performance plus (iii) it improves employee retention. Examples of Employee Engagement KPIs [59] that you can adapt to your organisation include:

- employee retention/turnover
- employee net promoter score
- employee absenteeism
- employee happiness
- client happiness
- ratings on Glassdoor website.

True potential can be achieved through motivation, but each person is different; therefore, the motivational triggers will differ accordingly. It can be challenging to apply a singular motivational trigger to every employee.

To give you an example of how employees can be motivated, I will share the example used at Thomson Reuters. They *"encourage… employees to be curious and challenge the status quo. We also focus on ensuring we have an environment of trust and openness, where our employees can feel safe to take interpersonal and ideational risks"*.[60] They have published a list of motivational triggers used throughout their organisation. Here are just some (not all):

- discovering innovative solutions
- constantly learning
- working with awesome people in an awesome culture
- enjoying flexibility
- having fun
- helping other employees to succeed
- sharing knowledge
- challenging the status quo
- solving puzzles
- empowering other employees.

Think about the motivational triggers that you can employ within your organisation.

5.4.   The mental process of decision making

Many organisations lack clarity on the decision-making process, specifically, the types of decisions to be made and by whom.

The decision-making process is influenced by the decision-maker's intrinsic and extrinsic motivational triggers. The motivational triggers will encourage people to act, but it does not set the pathway forward on taking action without a decision-making process. Our decision-making is based on cognitive biases hidden in our motivational triggers. Cognitive biases help us make choices.

Those choices must be objective and make sense because sometimes, our decisions are made instantly without considering the immediate and future implications.

Professor of Strategy at the University of Oxford, Thomas C. Powell, suggests that diligence-based strategy provides an applied method for developing, implementing and executing strategy. This diligence-based strategy helps managers overcome cognitive biases and illustrates how they can leverage management discipline and technology to drive increased performance and improve competitive advantage and growth within their organisations.[61] The competitive environment across all industries is forcing managers to make fast decisions. During the COVID-19 pandemic, managers worldwide had to make rapid decisions regarding their employees, supply chain, and customers for basic business survival. During times of crisis, taking the typical recognised strategic approach to decision-making will not work because it is too time-consuming. The research and analysis of trends are more prone to errors, and thus your decision-making can be flawed. The application of diligence-based activities allows you to focus on the activities that matter the most and lead to business success. For example, focus on a smaller number of business activities or switch to types of business activities that can be easily managed and still provide for customers, suppliers and employees.

5.5.   Motivation is the social process of influencing others

Motivation has always been generally considered to fulfil hunger, thirst, warmth and other needs. However, as human beings, it is also essential that we can meet our needs for social engagement, otherwise known as social motivation. Neuroscientist Antonia Hamilton places her perspective on what is meant by "social motivation." She describes social motivation as the need for "motivation to engage with other people, to interact with other people".[62] We recognise our need to be socially relevant and recognised with examples of love, friendship, safety, achievement, affiliation, approval and power.

The theory of social influence was first introduced by Kelman in 1958. Kelman stated that other people as individuals or groups could influence a person's beliefs, attitudes, behaviours and actions through three processes, namely (i) compliance, (ii) identification, and (iii) internalisation.

Further to Kelman's theory of social influence, a psychology teacher at The University of Manchester, Saul Mcleod, puts social influence into four categories:[63]

1. Majority Influence (Conformity) occurs when there is a change in behaviour or belief of social behaviour.
2. Compliance influence occurs when an individual disagrees with the group's beliefs, behaviour, or actions but agrees publicly.
3. Obedience occurs when an individual follows the direction of an authorised person.
4. Minority Influence takes place when a small group (minority) can influence the people in a larger group (majority).

Understanding the concept of social influence in your organisation will enable you to push the relevant motivational triggers for each employee.

5.6.   Personality types and traits

Personality types and traits differ among all human beings, and it is essential to understand these types and traits. The Myers-Briggs Personality Type Indicator lists the 16 most common types of different personality types and traits. The coding for the different types [64] is broken down as follows:

EXRTAVERSION (E) – INTROVERSION (I)
SENSING (S) – INTUITION (N)
THINKING (T) – FEELING (F)
JUDGING (J) – PERCEIVING (P)

If a person is, for example, recognised as being of personality type ESFJ, then, when looking at the Myers-Briggs coding, that person would be considered to have a personality that consists of extraversion, sensing, feeling and judging.

Respected author Heidi Priebe reviews the different types of personalities and traits:[65]

ISTJ – No one else is going to complete the task unless that person completes it.

ISTP – Tell the person about the available shortcut to get the task accomplished.

ISFJ – A task is relied upon to be completed by a person, i.e. the responsibility falls upon their shoulders to get the task completed.

ISFP – Tell the person that only creative people can complete the task.

INFJ – You need a person's insight into getting the task completed.

INFP – A task needs to be completed uniquely.

INTJ – You are the best person to complete the task because no other person can figure out the way.

INTP – Tell the person that the present methods are inaccurate.

ESTP – Tell the person that they are the only capable person of completing the task.

ESTJ – Tell the person the immediate and tangible benefits.

ESFP – Tell the person how other people will be impressed by their accomplishments.

ESFJ – Tell the person that their loved one needs it to be completed.

ENFP – Making people believe that it is them that can accomplish the task.

ENFJ – A person's guidance is needed to accomplish the task.

ENTP – Making people believe that something cannot be done.

ENTJ – Tell the person about the long-term benefits of completing the task.

As a manager or leader, understanding these different personality types and traits will enable you to pursue the best motivational strategies to effect change in your employees' behaviour patterns. Firstly, based upon the Myers-Briggs Personality Type Indicator, you need to identify your personality type. Which indicator best fits your personality? Secondly, identify the personality types and traits of your team. What can you do to increase your team's motivational behaviour?

Chapter Summary

The leaders and managers need to develop a culture that consistently motivates the team and employees. This culture needs to be enhanced by all employees within the organisation, not just a select few employees. Brian Tracy, motivational public speaker and self-development author, states that the culture can only be developed and maintained through creating a collaborative environment. Financial reward is one motivational factor, but more importantly, employees will perform their best work when they see that their efforts are recognised. Employees need to feel that their tireless efforts contribute to the organisation's goals; otherwise, they will not get motivated.

Feedback given to employees in a positive, constructive manner (not just words) will help to keep employees motivated. Negative feedback to employees is damaging to the organisation and the employee.

Each employee will have a different work style, personality and traits. You need to be aware of how to manage their different types to achieve the best performance from them. You need to lead by example.

6. Change in organisations and groups

Inside each organisation, you will find groups and teams of employees. This chapter examines how the factors surrounding an organisation make it unique and how, when an organisation undergoes simple or radical changes, these groups need to be able to accept the change before implementation.

5.1   What is an organisation?

Let's get a good understanding of what is an organisation. There are many different interpretations of the definition of 'organisation', but the central definition is *"a collection of resources that are working together somehow to achieve a common purpose"*.[66] However, aside from businesses, there are other types of organisations, such as the family unit and sporting teams. Therefore, put simply, an organisation can be defined as a group of people pursuing a particular objective(s).[67]

Our guide focuses on business organisations that possess a group of human resources. Human resources aim to satisfy a common purpose of meeting the goals.

To achieve its goals, an organisation must utilise its resources (capital and human) effectively and determine its processes. The processes of an organisation can be performed in five steps [67] as described below:

1. Determining the activities of the organisation.
2. Segregating the activities into workable areas such as departments or groups.
3. The placement of authority and responsibility on the leader of the group to ensure that the designated activities are performed.
4. The development of relationships between the group leader and their employees.
5. Creation of supervising lines which are enhanced through the development of policies.

Organisation structure

Within any organisation, you will find a particular structure that best fits that organisation. The most common type of formal structure that best defines an organisation [67] is:

LINE ORGANISATION. The flow of the authority starts from the leader or manager and flows through to the bottom level of the organisation.

FUNCTIONAL ORGANISATION. The organisation will consist of multiple departments. Each department will have sub-departments. The authority starts within each department (the function) and flows through from the leader to the lowest level of structure within the department.

The influencing factors that make an organisation unique

A common question frequently asked is how to make an organisation unique. The uniqueness of your organisation will depend upon many factors that you should consider, such as:

- Size of the organisation. The management of change is less complex in a smaller organisation. As the organisation grows, behavioural change management becomes more complex as you have to cope with an increased workforce and increased business activities. There are more employees and their different behavioural patterns to manage.
- The organisation's personality (culture). Does your organisation operate with a rigid formal practice, or is the organisation less formal (informal)? How do the employees rate the culture of the organisation? If the employees' culture rating is low, you will need to consider implementing changes to the culture to improve productivity and performance. Implementing positive changes to improve the culture will reduce some of the negative behavioural patterns within the organisation.
- Leadership style. The leadership style of the leaders and managers will dictate the success or failure of change within an organisation. There are two types of leadership (i) participative and (ii) autocratic. The participative leadership style allows management to include employees in the decision-making process on a consensus basis. The autocratic leadership style presents decisions being made at the top level of the organisation with no input from employees.
- The organisation's life cycle. Different life cycles of an organisation mean different objectives and goals to be achieved. Consequently, organisations will operate differently to changes and achievement of goals.[68]

What is VUCA?

Over the decades, the way businesses operate has changed...dramatically. Work lives are fast-paced (often hectic!), and with an increasingly connected society enabled by technology, we often find ourselves in unforeseeable situations.

The internet, smartphones, and social media allow us instant access to global events: the COVID-19 pandemic, the conflict in Ukraine, etc. increasing our sense of turmoil and uncertainty. We no longer feel secure, stable and sure of the future.

Such situations are summed up using VUCA, a managerial acronym for volatility, uncertainty, complexity, and ambiguity.[69][70] It perfectly describes the constant, unpredictable change many now experience in the workplace, especially in specific industries and business genres.

Adopting the VUCA method steers you away from the more traditional (often outdated) approaches to management and leadership in the workplace.

VOLATILITY. Like financial markets that experience volatility, organisations should be ready for unpredictable change. Organisations should be able to react immediately to the uncertainty.

UNCERTAINTY. The future is never certain.

COMPLEXITY. Chaos and confusion can occur when the change is complex.

AMBIGUITY. The change or situation lacks clarity.

In today's business environment, the norm is to expect a fast-paced and unpredictable change, as we saw during the COVID-19 pandemic and the earlier global financial crisis. Unpredictable change can be a result of internal or external forces. It can happen across all departments (internal), all organisations (internal and external) and all industry sectors (external) at any time. An organisation can face constant unpredictable changes, and it needs to be alert and ready for these changes. Therefore, the traditional approach to daily working practices, decision making, and leadership styles need to be discarded as they are no longer working or effective in today's environment.

Organisations should continually update their approach to managing change with their available resources (human and capital) and expect the unexpected.

To manage VUCA in today's business environment, the team at MindTools [69] have put forth problem areas that you will need to recognise in your organisation. Some of the many problem areas highlighted by the team at MindTools include:

- the loss of motivation
- destabilises career opportunities
- employees and management become more anxious
- a greater chance of bad decisions being made
- the decision-making process becomes paralysed
- the success of change can be jeopardised.

6.2. Homan's theory of group formation

Any organisation undertaking group formation is exposed to significant risk, plus the group formation can be unreliable and unpredictable.[71]

One of the best theories on group formation is the Homan's Theory, developed by George Homans, president of the American Sociological Association, member of Harvard's Department of Social Relations, and Chairman of Harvard's Department of Sociology. His theory was based upon "*the more activities persons share, the more numerous will be their interactions and the stronger will be their shared activities and sentiments, and the more sentiments people have for one another, the more will be their shared activities and interactions*".[72] Homan states that the group's behaviour and the outcome are based upon the interaction between the group and the environment. His theory linked the relationships between activities, interactions and sentiment, as illustrated in Figure 3.

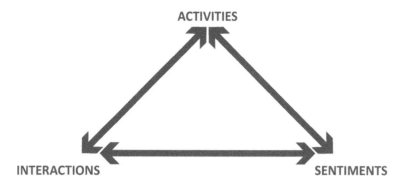

(The interdependence of Activities, Interactions and Sentiments)

Figure 3: Homan's theory on group formation

Homan also states that the group will go through many behavioural stages based on being influenced by the environment, as shown in Figure 4.

Figure 4: Behavioural Changes

Homan indicates that five factors will influence the behavioural changes – (i) physical restraints, (ii) cultural, (iii) technology resources and facilities, (iv) policies and procedures and (v) socio-economic factors.

Homan puts forward how you can put his theory to good practice in your organisation:[73]

- performance can be improved by removing any physical restraints
- instil a set of values and beliefs and make your team aware
- conduct a SWOT Analysis and PESTLE Analysis to identify the factors that can impact the change within the organisation
- the team and you are not acting in isolation
- make effective use of resources by training your team on what resources are available and how these resources should be used.

6.3. Purpose of groups

A group comprises two or more employees and has a common intent – to achieve the organisation's objectives.[74] There are four types of groups: formal, informal, committees and command groups.[75]

FORMAL GROUPS. The formal group is based upon activities that have to be completed and are designed to achieve specific objectives within the group and for the organisation. For example, many publicly listed organisations worldwide will have an audit and risk group. The establishment of this formal group has the achieved objectives of managing risk and reducing the potential of fraud.

The size of the group needs to be considered critically. Too many employees within the group can disrupt the performance and effectiveness of the group. The size of the group should be dependent on the activities required to be completed without excess employees.

Decision-making within groups is generally easier to make, providing all group members are involved with the collaboration of challenges, ideas and solutions. However, peer pressure within a group (subgroup) can disrupt the ease of decision making.

INFORMAL GROUPS. Informal groups are social. The employees usually form these groups to increase their desire for social interaction.

COMMITTEES. Committees can be formed drawing upon employees from different groups and can be temporary or permanent. The committees will have objectives that are to be achieved. For example, the corporate governance committee may be formed to ensure that the organisation acts transparently to its stakeholders and the public. This committee may draw upon employees from human resources, finance, manufacturing and marketing departments.

COMMAND GROUPS. Generally known as a task group, this group has to perform one activity, such as a product launch, and the group members will come from different formal groups. After the task has been completed, the employees will return to their previous formal group.

Peer group pressure

In the virtual world (not the real world), peer group pressure is a stronger driver of behaviour.[2] Peer group pressure can be seen in the virtual world through a presence on online social media platforms. Customers and employees are prime examples of peer group pressure applied to organisations. Customers can offer positive or negative feedback on an organisation's product or service by commenting on online social media platforms. Potential customers can review this positive or negative feedback to make their own decisions regarding purchasing the product or service.

Similarly, employees can rate their own working experience with an organisation through online platforms such as Indeed. Organisations can learn from this feedback to improve their culture, leadership styles and working practices to attract new employees. Too much negative feedback from peer groups of employees will indicate to potential employees that the organisation is not a good place to be working.

6.4. Groups versus teams

A group and a team are different in many ways. The best way to illustrate these differences between groups and teams is to illustrate the differences. [76]

Group	Team
Individual goals	Shared goals
Individual accountability	Individual and mutual accountability
Individual success or failure	Collective success or failure

Figure 5: Difference between groups and teams

6.5. Agile teams

An agile team is a small group of people that have been assigned to complete a task or project.[77] Agile teams are continuously planning throughout the project's life rather than making the initial plan at the beginning of the project. The use of an agile team provides the added benefit of flexibility within the project as the agile team is constantly making adjustments as changes to the project arise. To build a high-performing agile team within an organisation, managers and leaders must first accept the agile mindset plus have the best team based on their knowledge, skills, experience, and values.

6.6. Five stages of a group development

A change within an organisation requires effort, strategy, time and performance by groups or teams. Bruce Tuckman, a psychologist, illustrated the five stages that, over time, groups would move through to increase effectiveness. Tuckman mentions that the five stages include (i) forming, (ii) storming, (iii) norming, (iv) performing, and (v) adjourning. [71] However, not all groups manage to succeed through the five stages and will get stuck somewhere in the life cycle due to not being able to solve the problems or address the differences. Marija Kojic, a productivity writer, illustrates the life cycle of the five stages (refer to Figure 6) based on the group's effectiveness over time.

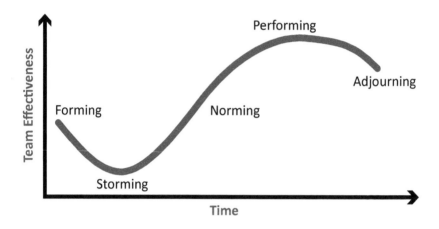

Figure 6: Five stages of group development

On the next pages I have listed the five stages that influence organisational behaviour amongst groups (Table 9).

STAGES	DETAILS [78] [79]
Forming	This stage involves group orientation. At this early stage, the group members are getting to know everyone else, and they are being polite to each other. The change or the project is exciting because it is new. The group members may be feeling nervous. During this stage, the group leader will likely be appointed. They start to form work patterns, and all group members get to see each other's work patterns
Storming	This stage discusses the power struggle within the organisation. The group members will likely lose their politeness as they are in the second stage. This stage shows that the individual group members are likely to express their opinions and exchange ideas. This may lead to unnecessary interpersonal conflicts, disputes and power struggles You may see the group divide itself into subgroups, thus preventing group cohesion based on different ideas and opinions. It is okay to have the storming stage in your organisation as it allows all views, opinions, and ideas to be aired rather than swept under the carpet
Norming	This stage is cooperation, integration, and unity. This stage is less hostile than the storming stage. The group is in positive mode, and the group leaders can witness a productivity and performance increase during this stage. Interaction between group members becomes significantly easier
Performing	This stage is characterised by overall synergy. Synergy is achieved as the group and its members are well-organised and focused on making the change a success by achieving the organisation's goals

STAGES	DETAILS [78] [79]
Adjourning	This stage is the closure of the project or change. If the closure relates to a project, then on the completion of the project, the group may be dissolved, and this may cause mourning between group members after they have built up a relationship with other members. The group is likely to remain operational after a change within the organisation has been implemented

Table 9: Five Stages of Group Development

Leaders and managers must know which stage their groups are going through.

6.7. Making groups perform

Making groups perform in the workplace can be challenging. Groups have different behavioural patterns and work ethics. If an organisation has multiple groups, work ethics and behavioural patterns may vary from group to group. Groups working to their maximum capacity will enable a greater chance of success with changes. Group working improves the opportunity for better learning, greater synergies, improved motivation levels, increased productivity and improved efficiencies for the group(s) and the organisation.

How do you maximise the operational performance of each group in your organisation? I have compiled a list of tips put together by respected authors in the industry (Table 10). You can start to apply these tips in your organisation today.[80][81]

IMPROVING GROUP PERFORMANCE TIPS

1. Set clear goals and communicate these goals to all members so that they are aware of the outcome expected

2. Establish the guidelines on how the group will operate, including leadership, roles, responsibilities and work ethics

3. Understand each member's strengths, weaknesses, work ethics, skills, experience and opinions

4. The change in the organisation needs to be planned from start to finish concerning resources needed, timing and allocation of responsibilities. Brainstorm the change in the group to assess challenges, and develop ideas and plans. This stage requires contribution from all members of the group

5. Determine the length of time needed to complete the change

6. Allocation of tasks to each member, so they are aware of their responsibility plus shared understanding between all group members. The allocation of tasks must be accompanied by time limits as other tasks may rely upon certain tasks to be completed before they can start

7. Encourage communications within the group between a leader and members plus members to other members within the group

8. Conduct regular meetings to discuss progress and, if necessary, reassign tasks or change the timeline for tasks

9. Monitor the progress of the organisation's change

10. After completing the change, a final meeting should be held within the groups. The meeting needs to cover the success or failure of the change: what could have been done better and improvements required for the future

Table 10: Tips to improve group work performance

6.8. How to manage the change in the group

It is important to manage the change within the group from the start to the finish of the project.

Randy Conley, a Top 100 Leadership Speaker & Thinker, provide helpful advice and strategies that you can use in your organisation to help your team manage change.[82] He recommends the following six strategies should be adopted to manage change in the group:

1. Help the group and its members understand the need for change.
2. Actively engage the group and its members in planning the change.
3. If group members have concerns, it is important to address their concerns upfront.
4. Give autonomy to the group to make adjustments to their plans as deemed appropriate so that they can achieve the outcome.
5. Develop emotional moments so that the team can feel the emotion.
6. Encourage feedback throughout the process of change. This feedback may adjust the course taken to achieve the change.

> **"In a world that's changing quickly, the only strategy that is guaranteed to fail is not taking risks."**
> *Mark Zuckerberg, Facebook*
>
> And he was right. Leadership is not a static endeavour. Successful managers not only acknowledge the need for business development but also are willing and able to navigate their team through change."[180]

Chapter Summary

This chapter has outlined the types of organisations and the four groups that will fit into the different types of organisations. Groups are formed to achieve the goals of the organisation. There is a significant difference between groups and teams in how they operate and the type of goals to be achieved. Groups that are formed go through a life cycle of five stages before they are dissolved or continue with a new change.

For an organisation to successfully achieve the desired outcomes of a change, the leaders and managers must manage the groups during change and ensure the group can perform the change. The strategies illustrated at the end of the chapter can be used in your organisation. Changes will frequently occur as the business environment continually changes.

7. Key challenges in organisational change and how to fix them

In all organisations, change will be inevitable, and the change will appear in many forms. Some people within the organisation will be receptive to the change, but others will be overwhelmingly resistant. The most common reasons why people resist change include (i) the fear of the unknown, (ii) they do not see the benefits arising from the change for themselves, (iii) lack of trust, (iv) poor communication, (v) emotions and (vi) fear of failure. The people who resist change may be individuals, teams or groups within your organisation.

This chapter exposes some of the key challenges organisations face towards change and suggests recommendations to overcome the challenges. When an organisation is planning to make a change, regardless of the size of the change or industry sector, leaders and managers should plan and anticipate employee resistance to the change.

7.1. The 6 key challenges/blockers of organisational change

Organisations will change constantly, and they need to be prepared for the challenges ahead, including resistance to the change, by ensuring adequate planning. As a manager or leader, you are uniquely positioned to anticipate the challenges and include solutions in your plan. The anticipation and minimisation of these challenges will mitigate disruption and improve the chances of successful change.[83]

You may ask yourself, why does this matter? It matters because your organisation will have a greater chance of meeting its goals with a good change management strategy. If your organisation lacks a change management strategy, it's unlikely you will achieve your goals. Similarly, a poor management strategy means the change will lack cohesion. You are not likely to achieve the goals and will face unexpected barriers with no idea how to overcome them.

Let's look at some key blockers and challenges towards change faced by organisations today. Kadabra and Prosci list the main barriers faced and put forth their solutions to overcome these barriers (refer to Table 11). [83][84]

NO.	BARRIER	RECOMMENDATION
1	Individual Change Resistance. The resistance may arise from a new process, strategy or organisational structure. The change resistance is not just limited to individuals. Teams or groups within your organisation may be resistant to the change	Leaders and managers must be able to anticipate resistance, and thus the anticipated resistance must form part of the planning process to minimise potential disruption to the change plan. There is a need to encourage employee buy-in

NO.	BARRIER	RECOMMENDATION
2	Communication is poor. In some cases, there is no communication	Two-way communication within any organisation is essential. When an organisation changes, communication is vital throughout the planning and implementation stage
3	No strategic direction or lack thereof	There must be a clear definition of the goals that need to be achieved from the change. There needs to be a clear strategy drawn up that will provide the roadmap on how the change will be driven and how the goals will be achieved
4	Lack of consistency. Each person has a different set of beliefs, ideas and behavioural patterns, and these may contradict with other persons (known as cognitive dissonance), thus providing inconsistency with the manner in how activities or change should be implemented	Management must gain a fast understanding of each person who is involved in the implementation to pinpoint any consistencies that may occur. Encourage your implementation team to speak out and provide solutions to improve consistency between expectations and actual outcomes
5	Cultural barriers arising from the inclusion of diverse groups. This barrier can occur within an organisation with a single operation or multiple operations worldwide	Understanding each person involved with the change and what they care about most. Do not alienate people or groups within your organisation. Actively involve them with the planning and organisation of change

NO.	BARRIER	RECOMMENDATION
6	The perception is that the leadership are not buying into the organisation's change	The top management needs to be involved in the activities associated with the organisation change
7	Lack of investment and resourcing (human and capital). This barrier can arise from insufficient planning and not knowing the requirements	From a human resourcing perspective, careful planning needs to be undertaken by management

Table 11: Seven Most Common Barriers to Organisation Change

7.2. Influence of leadership in organisational change

Impact of leadership

An organisation with a good culture can manage change with greater success. An organisation that suffers from an adverse culture will incur more significant barriers and resistance to change.

Leaders and managers experience the same physical and emotional success and failures as others. They are not immune to the expectations and requirements of stakeholders (including employees), and they provide the leadership needed to steer an organisation towards achieving its goals.

Leadership directly affects an organisation's culture, and it is up to leaders to demonstrate the values and beliefs to all employees.[85] Leadership is critical in developing the best-fit culture within an organisation. The foundation of culture can be used to cultivate leadership. This process occurs through the empowerment of employees to achieve the company mission and realise how vital each of their contributions is to accomplish the task.

AlignOrg Solutions cited a survey conducted on leadership and change management.[86] Elements from the survey showed that 87% of leaders trained their managers on the change process. The managers implemented the change, but the change did not last. The result shows that only 22% of those surveyed reflected that the training was effective.[87] There were five reasons put forth to state why the training on change management became ineffective:[86]

1. The managers' mindset failed to adopt the change management mentality.
2. The managers failed to manage the change effectively and let the change manage them.
3. The managers did not fully understand their team and individuals' mindsets.
4. The managers failed to gain the employees' support.
5. The managers did not hold their teams and individuals accountable.

Negative impact on change management

Leaders and managers should always be prepared for change. Change has become a constant factor within any organisation, and communication is critical to reducing the negative impact of change. Therefore, leaders must buy into the change, engage with it, and effectively communicate the change to their managers and employees.

Failure of leaders to buy into the change and positively participate in the change will drop employee morale.[88] Employees seek guidance and leadership from their leaders. They will not engage with organisational change, nor will they have a positive mindset toward the change if leaders do not buy into and communicate it.

7.3.   Leadership styles

You may be surprised to learn that leadership is within everyone. However, I will quantify that by saying there is a difference between a leader and an effective leader and it is determined by leadership style. Many variables come to play in determining leadership style. It will vary from person to person and can change within a manager or leader depending upon their current emotional state or health. A manager can usually offer good leadership to employees, but their leadership style may suffer if the leader or manager is suffering from health issues or negative emotional feelings. Also, a person's leadership style must be flexible to accommodate changes in the organisation's short, mid and long-term goals.

Understanding your leadership style will help you overcome the pitfalls of that particular leadership style. Let's briefly look at the four most common leadership styles as described in Table 12:[89]

LEADERSHIP STYLE	ADVANTAGES	DISADVANTAGES
Autocratic	• faster decision-making • performance can be improved	• the presence of fear and resentment • if the leader is not present, the organisation can be paralysed
Democratic	• employees at all levels are involved in the decision-making • happier working environment	• decision making is slower • leaders can become too dependent upon the employees and not be able to make their own decisions
Transformational	• growth in trust in the leader from the employees • improved balancing of short and long-term goals	• the implementation of change may not be strongly detailed for employees to follow

LEADERSHIP STYLE	ADVANTAGES	DISADVANTAGES
Laissez-faire (The team self-directs the change)	• improves employee retention • improves accountability • employees can react to changes quickly	• the increased stress levels for employees as they have to make decisions • less accountability for their actions

Table 12: Types of Leadership Styles

Leadership styles

There are many other leadership styles. Other leadership styles include (i) strategic, (ii) transactional, (iii) bureaucratic and (iv) coach-style.[90]

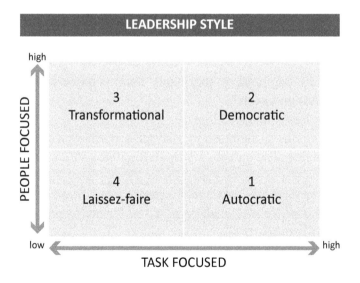

Figure 7: Leadership styles

What is your leadership style?

Do you want to see what type of leadership style you own? I have compiled some questions below to help you decide.

1. **If you find serious conflict within your team, what action do you take? Do you...**
   A. Give your team a subtle reminder that there are goals that have to be met.
   B. Call a team meeting to discuss the conflict.
   C. Do nothing, hoping that the conflict will go away.

2. **Do you trust your team members?**
   A. I have total trust in my team members.
   B. An average level of trust.
   C. Nope! I do not trust them at all.

3. **Noting that some of your team members are highly skilled and motivated, what do you do?**
   A. Be flexible and let them utilise their skills.
   B. Do nothing.
   C. Tell the team members that they have to follow the organisation's processes and procedures.

3. **How do you ensure that your team members achieve the organisation's goals?**
   A. Be a leader and lead from the front
   B. Encourage all members to participate in achieving the goals
   C. Delegate tasks and not follow up with team members

Once you have answered all the above questions, take a moment to see how you can improve your leadership to best fit your employees and the organisation's culture.

7.4.   Importance of corporate governance

Corporate governance

Corporate governance plays a vital role in assisting organisations to be sustainable and to be able to achieve their long-term objectives. It starts with the Board of Directors, who establish the framework and are responsible for ensuring the corporate governance framework is implemented throughout the organisation by all employees.

Corporate governance is the framework that sets out the policies, rules, internal controls and processes on how the organisation will be directed and controlled.[91] Corporate governance is designed to improve accountability, independence, fairness and transparency to all stakeholders, including shareholders, customers, suppliers and employees.[91]

Leadership plays an essential role in a change initiative

Corporate governance requires positive and effective leadership. Sarah Bell, a partner at Grant Thornton (UK), is quoted as saying that *"the art of good governance is about working smarter, not harder, by taking a principles-based approach to achieving your objectives and aligning your business model to the interests of all stakeholders in the organisation"*. [92] To achieve good governance, an organisation must have the best systems to prevent fraud and mismanagement, including checks and balances. However, the checks and balances must be strong enough to be transparent to stakeholders but not so rigid that they prevent the organisation from achieving its strategic objectives. Having the systems in place for the best corporate governance is meaningless unless these systems are constantly monitored and reported to deliver excellence in corporate governance to all stakeholders. Monitoring of the outcomes from the systems will identify areas needed for improvement. The Board of Directors should receive constant communication on the effectiveness and outcomes of the corporate governance systems.

The organisation's profile, core values, strategies and culture must be established as part of its corporate governance. Leadership is responsible for ensuring that the values, strategy and culture are embedded throughout the organisation in all communications and activities from the top level downwards. Bell [92] points out that there are some qualities that leaders should adopt, including:

1. To ensure that the organisation has an effective board of directors or leadership team who can set the tone to provide direction and guidance towards the strategic goals.
2. The core values must be visible and realistic. The core values must be embedded throughout the organisation. The core values must be embedded in its culture as this has a direct impact on behaviour.
3. The organisation's strategic goals must be aligned with the business model.

The need for change governance

International speaker, bestselling author and co-founder of Being First, Dr Linda Ackerman, states that organisations must have effective change governance in place to manage their change.[93] Even though an organisation may have best practice corporate governance systems for their existing business model, she states that leaders often fail to incorporate corporate governance into their change initiatives. Some of these change initiatives may have been forced upon an organisation, particularly during the COVID-19 pandemic when strategies had to be quickly redesigned. Implementing these strategies was quick and corporate governance may have been overlooked.

Without effective change governance, an organisation may expect delays in the change initiative due to a lack of communication among leaders throughout the change and who is responsible for making decisions.

Bell outlines four elements of best practice change governance: [92]

1. Leadership roles must be clearly defined, communicated and coached.
2. A change leadership structure that takes control of the change initiative.
3. A clear pathway of the process and responsibility for decision making.
4. The relationship must be clearly defined between the people leading the change initiative and the people running the operation.

7.5. The 6 steps to unblock resistance to change

The concluding part of this chapter examines the basic steps you can adopt in your organisation to unblock the resistance to change. In any organisation, you must be mindful that the employees will decide if adapting to change will serve their purpose and benefit them.[7] There are many reasons individual employees and groups may become resistant to change, such as fear, depression, venturing into the unknown, denial, shock and frustration. However, Kotter and Schlesinger have identified four reasons people resist change:[94]

1. Self-interest is dominant.
2. Due to misunderstanding.
3. People suffer from a low tolerance to change.
4. Employees will derive their assessments about the change.

Prosci mentions that resistance has to be managed effectively if an organisation wants to make a change.[95] The organisation has compiled a list of best practices in change management based on its research over the last two decades. The best practices in change management for your consideration include:

- you have only one attempt to do the change management, and it must be correct the first time
- you must be aware that there will be resistance to change
- resistance should be addressed formally
- the root causes of resistance must be identified
- engage resistance managers who can quickly handle the resistance.

Kotter and Schlesinger have compiled a list of approaches to help you unblock these barriers to change (known as the Six Change Approaches). [96]

1. **Education and communication.** Education about the change should occur before the change takes place. Communication is critical. It is better to over-communicate than not to communicate.
2. **Participation and involvement.** Involve the team, including those employees that could potentially resist the change. The team can participate in designing the change, which will give them ownership.
3. **Facilitation and support.** Provide each team member with emotional support, education, and training to help them manage the change.
4. **Negotiation and agreement.** Employees who are resistant to change can be offered a financial incentive to overcome their resistance. However, this approach is biased towards employees who are resistant to change and unfair to those who are not resistant to the change. Any financial incentive should include all employees involved in the change.
5. **Manipulation and co-optation.** This approach seems unethical, but it may be the only alternative available if all other approaches fail.
6. **Explicit and implicit coercion.** This approach involves threatening employees and teams to undertake the change. The threats can consist of rewards being withdrawn or losing their jobs if they do not accept the change.

Chapter Summary

Change in your organisation will be inevitable, and you cannot escape change unless you do not want to grow your organisation. There will be employees or teams resistant to change whilst others will be receptive to change.

This chapter has outlined the blockers to organisational change and has provided you with tips that you can use to overcome these blockers. Strong and effective leadership are essential factors that will help minimise these barriers.

Don't forget to identify your leadership style by taking the quiz.

8. Managing conflict in your organisation

Conflict is disruptive in any organisation. Conflicts slow down efficiency and productivity whilst decreasing morale can cause an organisation to lose its competitive advantage, harm brand equity, and potentially lose profits if the conflict is not suitably managed in a short period. Conflicts cannot be prevented, but occurrences can be minimised with the right fit culture and appropriate strategies.

This chapter delves into the strategies that will fit most organisations (small or large) to manage change and suggests solutions to manage conflicts. Firstly, Lewin's Three-Stage Model for Change is explained to help you change the status-quo within your organisation (to make change work). Secondly, conflict resolution strategies are covered, along with managing conflict in your Workplace. A change can quickly become short-term if mechanisms are not developed to keep the new status-quo as the new norm, so the chapter concludes with how to make the change sustainable.

8.1.   Lewin's Three-Stage Model of Change

Kurt Lewin, a social psychologist and a leader in change management, developed a 3 Stage Model of Change. The concept relating to the development of this change model was to study the areas of (i) the change process in an organisation's environment and (ii) how the status-quo could be challenged to make changes more effective. The best way to summarise this three-stage model is via illustration, as shown in Figure 8.[97]

In brief, the model functions to understand the present situation and initiate a change process that will lead to a future state. Lewin identifies that the group's behaviour towards change enforces an individual's behaviour. Therefore the stages rely upon the group's behaviour *and* the individuals within the group.

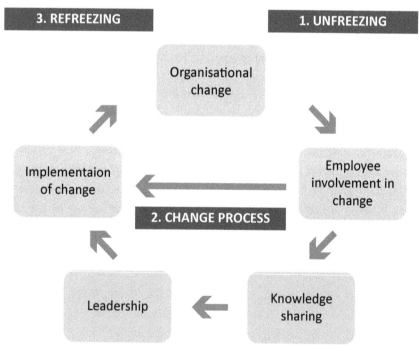

Figure 8: Lewin's 3 Stage Model of Change

Let's take a moment to delve deeper into the three stages of Lewin's model.

STAGE ONE: UNFREEZING

In his Force Field Analysis model, Lewin identifies two types of forces that can come into play during the "unfreezing" stage. The two types of forces (refer to Figure 9) that are evident at this stage are (i) restraining forces (resistance to the change) and (ii) driving forces (positive forces for the change).[98] When an organisation wants to move from its present state to the desired state, these forces come into play.

LEWIN FORCE FIELD ANALYSIS

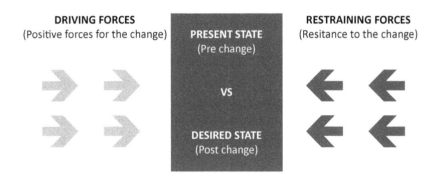

Figure 9: Lewin's Force Field Analysis

Concerning any change, Lewin states that human behaviour acts in a "quasi-stationary equilibrium state." At this stage, the mental and physical capacity of an individual's mindset can be reached but is not typically attained. Therefore, if the group is resistant to change, Lewin states that this behaviour has to be unfrozen for the group to be open to organisational change.

Adopting Lewin's Force Field Analysis Model, Table 13 shows some common forces that leaders and managers are likely to face. To oppose these restraining forces to change and gain support, the leaders and managers should implement the driving forces.

RESTRAINING FORCES FROM GROUPS OR INDIVIDUALS	DRIVING FORCES TO COUNTERACT THE RESTRAINING FORCES
Employees do not understand why there is a need for change	Leaders and managers need to explain the reasons for the change and how they will benefit
Worried that the change will create an additional work burden	Inform the group and people how their tasks will be simpler and improve their productivity and efficiency

Table 13: Lewin's Force Field Analysis Model

As Lewin states, "motivation for change must be generated before change can occur".[99] The unfreezing ("melting the ice") component will consist of determining what needs to be changed, the reasons to support why the change needs to be made, developing the need for change and being open to the group and individual concerns before starting the change process.

STAGE TWO: CHANGE PROCESS

The "unfreezing" stage is now complete.

Next, the change process needs to be planned well, with many options available: there is no guarantee that the change will be successful without considering options. By creating options, you can see what works and what does not by trial and error, plus evaluating the success or failure of each option. The change process must encourage openness through communication, involve the groups and individuals, plus empower these people to (a) be proactive and (b) take action. Rumours should be dispelled.

The evaluation process must consider the impact of the leadership during the change and the flow of information. Learn from the positive and the negative aspects of the change, i.e. what worked and what did not.

The "refreezing" process is designed to make the change sustainable. This process becomes the new "normal" (status-quo) for groups to accept. Groups no longer present resistance as the change has occurred and will be sustainable in the future.

Lewin's model presses the need for the "refreezing" process to occur. Failure to implement this "refreezing" process will result in groups going back to their old norms and behaviours, defeating the purpose of the change.

The "refreezing" process will need to implement formal and informal mechanisms so that the change can be frozen without disruption. As part of this process, leaders and managers must foster the following:

- Organisations need to identify change supports and barriers. Similarly, the changes should be built into the organisation's culture.
- Communicate and encourage openness.
- Ensure that the groups and people have access to the necessary training.
- Promote ways that the change is sustainable in the long term.

The final step in the "refreezing" process is to celebrate the success of the change.

8.2.   Conflict resolution strategies

Harvard Law School has compiled a list of conflict resolution strategies (refer to Table 14) that you can use in your organisation regardless of its size.[100]

NO.	STRATEGY	DETAIL OF THE STRATEGY
1	We possess biased fairness perceptions	Both parties in the conflict believe that they are right and that the other person is wrong. This conflict occurrence happens because of our perceptions. Both parties need to overcome these self-centred fairness perceptions, and there may be a need for a mediator to intervene in the conflict
2	Threats and provocative moves are to be avoided as this can escalate tensions	It is easy to be threatening in a conflict when you believe that you are correct. However, the issuance of threats or provocative moves will likely escalate the tensions and the conflict. Consider all other available options before issuing a threat to the other person
3	Do not indulge in the mentality of "us versus them."	This type of mentality aggravates the conflict. Groups tend to adopt this mentality as they have developed loyalty and strong relationships within the group. The group will view another group as a competitor and thus will not appreciate the other group's views and opinions Identify a common goal that the groups are trying to achieve. Highlight the similarities that exist between the groups. Smoothing of the conflict between the groups can occur as you grow the number of similarities between the groups

NO.	STRATEGY	DETAIL OF THE STRATEGY
4	Identify deeper issues that lie beneath the surface	One of the most common conflicts that arise relates to money. There are deeper issues that need to be examined before submitting to a pay increase to satisfy the conflict. Typically, the deeper issue lies with the fact that the employee has been overlooked or not respected within the organisation
5	Keep sacred from pseudo-sacred issues separate	The sacred values typically relate to non-negotiable values such as a person's religion. However, some of these sacred values can be pseudo-sacred values. The pseudo-sacred values become negotiable under certain conditions

Table 14: Conflict Resolution Strategies

8.3. Managing conflicts in the organisation

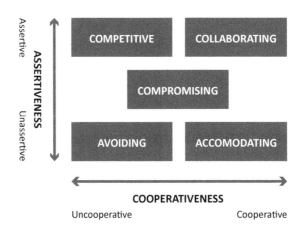

Figure 10: Thomas-Kilmann Conflict Mode Instrument

Styles of conflicts

Unhealthy conflicts within an organisation can easily get out of control if not contained quickly in the same manner as a house burning down without the aid of firefighters. Kenneth Thomas and Ralph Kilmann have identified five styles of conflict. These are summarised in the Thomas-Kilmann Conflict Mode Instrument (TKI), as illustrated in Figure 10.[101] There are two behaviours that a person can undertake – (i) being cooperative or (ii) being assertive.

Managing conflict can be responded to in five ways: [102]

1. **COMPETING.** This mode indicates that the person is highly uncooperative and highly assertive. A person will adopt this behaviour to obtain power.
2. **COLLABORATING.** A person is highly cooperative whilst being highly assertive at the same time.
3. **COMPROMISING.** This person displays a medium level of assertiveness and collaboration. This style indicates that the person seeks a win-win situation for themselves and other parties.
4. **AVOIDING.** The behavioural pattern and conflict style are opposite to the collaborating style. This person wants to avoid the conflict by not dealing with it or sidestepping it.
5. **ACCOMMODATING.** This person is highly cooperative but not assertive. This type of person is willing to satisfy the other party's needs without meeting their own needs.

Take a moment to examine the types of conflicts within your organisation.

Now that you have identified the types of conflicts, listed in Table 15 are some strategies you can employ to manage these conflicts. The UC San Diego has compiled a list of eight strategies that you may find helpful in your organisation.[103]

NO.	STRATEGY
1	Communicate with the other person
2	Focus on the person's behaviour
3	Listen to the other person
4	Identify agreement and disagreement areas
5	Prioritise conflict areas
6	Construct a plan to resolve the conflict
7	Take action on the plan
8	Build upon the success of resolving the conflict

Table 15: 8 strategies to manage conflict

8.4. Managing resistance to change

There must be a clear understanding of the underlying reasons that caused the conflict to arise. Once the conflict's causal reasons have been investigated, managing the conflict and resistance is critical to the organisation's success and satisfying all stakeholders. Managing the conflict involves resolving the conflict before it gets out of control.

Managing resistance to change requires that a leader or manager be responsive to the employees' needs providing that their needs have a foundation. If the employees' needs are not critical to the organisation's success, alternate measures need to be in place to remove the resistance.

Two decades of researching thousands of change management experts have allowed Prosci to provide five valuable tips on managing resistance (refer to Table 16).

PROSCI'S TIPS [104]	EXPLANATION
Change management has to be done right the first time There is normally no second chance	From the planning stage of the change project through to completion, leaders and managers must consider resistance by employees Leaders and managers must adopt a structured change management approach from the start. They must communicate, activate and engage throughout the change process. Employees are concerned about how they will benefit from the change
Expect that the change will bring resistance from teams and employees	Resistance to change is a psychological and physiological reaction. Each employee is different, so expect that their psychological and physiological reactions will differ Resistance should be foreseen at the early stage. Employees or teams will resist change if they are not informed and involved with the change. The reasons for resistance have already been stated
Formally address resistance to change	Resistance to change should not just be adopted when an organisation changes. Resistance management techniques should be burned into your organisation as part of your policies and procedures even when there is no change taking place Prosci identifies a three-phase approach to formally addressing resistance. The three phases are: [104] 1. Prepare 2. Manage 3. Sustain

PROSCI'S TIPS [104]	EXPLANATION
Discover the underlying problems of resistance	Leaders and managers need to discover the root causes of resistance. Managing the resistance to change becomes ineffective if the emphasis is on treating the symptoms only and not treating the root causes
Engage the best managers that can control resistance	Your organisation should employ the best resistance managers; managers that have the skills and experience to deal with resistance

Table 16: Prosci's tips on managing resistance

Once the resistance to conflict is resolved, the leader or manager will need to confirm that the employee is engaged and committed to the change. The employee should be monitored to ensure that the resistance to change has been dissolved.

8.5. Sustaining change

Sustaining change in the workplace can easily be managed, providing the early conflicts identified before and during the change were resolved. However, these (and new) conflicts could quickly arise in the post-change period.

Conflicts are inevitable because everyone is different, and conflict circumstances are often unique. However, many follow a similar pattern and should be studied closely to identify the factors surrounding them. Applying effective communication and listening are two ways that conflicts can be prevented.

Once the changes have been successfully implemented, they need to be sustainable for the long term. Sustaining change comes down to keeping the momentum going and managing potential threats before they arise. Organisations should have conflict prevention strategies to identify, monitor and treat conflicts before they escalate and blow out of control.

ACCIPIO, a UK leadership development service provider, suggests that organisations consider the following mannerisms that should be instilled into each person to avoid conflict and recommend that employees, including leaders and managers, adopt the following characteristics: [105]

- to be patient
- to be flexible
- to be respectful
- to avoid non-confrontational situations
- to avoid being judgemental
- to encourage openness
- to be a mindful listener
- to display positive body language
- to adopt a positive voice tone.

Chapter Summary

Before you can manage change in your organisation, Lewin's Three-Stage Model of Change should be used to understand the change process in an environment and challenge the status quo of the change so that it can become more effective.

There are different styles of conflicts that range between high and low levels of assertiveness and cooperativeness. Understanding the conflict style will assist you in your decision as to which conflict resolution strategy best fits the conflict. Be aware that the change process might incur resistance. This chapter has outlined ideas on managing resistance to change, and the final segment has guided how to make the change sustainable long-term in your organisation.

9. Life before COVID-19 and its impact on organisational behaviour

There are some important lessons that we can learn from unexpected change. This chapter looks at how a massive change such as COVID-19 was unexpectantly forced upon us. The lessons that we learn from this pandemic will shape organisations and how we do business collectively in the future.

9.1. Impact on business arising from COVID-19

Most organisations worldwide were conducting business as usual when the arrival of COVID-19 surprised us all. The pandemic struck like a tsunami, with many organisations being washed away because they were not prepared for such an event: companies were forced to close. Their closures will be permanent despite the massive financial packages provided by governments worldwide.

Of the many businesses fortunate to survive, their foundations were severely hit. The pandemic has changed the way businesses interact with their suppliers and customers,[106] and organisations across all industry sectors faced massive operational challenges. They had to find ways to overcome these challenges by finding new growth pathways while navigating through lockdowns, changing their product lines, and disrupting their supply chains and culture and employees. Businesses had to change their operational strategies, including developing the shift to a remote workforce.

Many companies were forced to change their business model to survive. If the operational models were not changed, the organisations would lose their customers because the supply chain and delivery channels had been severely disrupted.

Let's look at a classic example in the restaurant industry

Restaurants were forced to close their doors to their customers as customers could not dine in. Similarly, organisations could not hold board or staff meetings; therefore, restaurants were not required to cater for them. Many restaurant owners changed their business model simply by thinking "outside of the box." For example, providing takeaways and deliveries to the home.

In some cases, organisations had to change their product lines as the existing products would not have survived in the market due to changes in customers' needs and priorities. For example, organisations had to change their production lines to cater for the unsurprisingly increased demand for new medical products and supplies such as respirator masks, gowns, visors and swabs.[107] Many organisations adopted the change in product lines for two reasons: (i) to continue to make revenue and (ii) morally to help society remain safe during the pandemic.

Examples include:

LVMH converted its existing perfume production lines to make hand sanitisers.[108]

Foxconn, an iPhone manufacturer, changed its production line to make face masks.[109]

We must not forget that many organisations incurred additional, unplanned financial losses due to this pandemic, such as keeping employees safe in the workplace (or at home) and supplying new digital technology to stay in touch with their employees.

9.2. Impact on humans from the COVID-19 pandemic

We have seen how the COVID-19 pandemic has affected global business operations; now, let's take a look at how this pandemic has affected humans from a personal and work perspective.

Personal perspective

COVID-19 has had a devastating emotional and mental health impact on the human race. Millions of people were not fortunate enough to survive, and so many people worldwide have been infected or have come into contact with people infected with the virus.

The primary mental health issues that people have been impacted by include isolation, fear of losing their jobs, loss of income and bereavement. [110] Mental health issues are not easily recognised and often go untreated – a person may appear happy from their external appearance. However, no one can easily identify what is happening inside a person. People with mental health disorders need treatment before the disorder worsens.

People were left jobless and without income due to businesses being forced to close. Those people were forced into financial distress as they depended upon their employment income to pay for food, medical and utility bills. The United Nations predicted global unemployment would be over 200 million in 2022 due to COVID-19.[111]

A significant change is that since people have been forced into lockdown and working from home, the family unit has become more important in people's lives.[112]

Work perspective

Employees were forced to change their behavioural and activity patterns relating to how and where they worked. Situations were not chosen; they were imposed on the employees. Working from home gave birth to unfamiliar emotional feelings and behavioural patterns for many.

Recognising the important role managers need to play in understanding the change in human behaviour due to COVID-19, the team at Accenture suggests the new human behaviour will be known as the "New Human Experience." Five human implications can be expected from this new behavioural pattern,[113] as outlined in Table 17:

HUMAN IMPLICATIONS	DETAIL
Confidence comes with a cost	Confidence is expected to be eroded. The rebuilding of trust will be critical
Virtual century	All people will be affected by this pandemic in terms of communication and our social lives as transformation takes place to digital. The COVID-19 pandemic has fastened the pace of transformation to the virtual century faster than expected

HUMAN IMPLICATIONS	DETAIL
Health business will need to be part of an organisation's ecosystem	Accenture believes that organisations will need to expand their ecosystem to include health. The team believe that health experiences will be in demand
Cocooning	Due to the forced lockdowns, people were forced to work from home. People could balance their work and personal life better in many instances. People's lives became enriched as they did not have to travel to the office daily. Accenture believes that this cocooning around the home will be a premium feature in the future
Authority will be reinvented	The impact of lockdowns, self-isolation and limitations imposed upon travel will invigorate a change in authority. Authority is expected to be reverted to the top-down structure rather than a central authority

Table 17: New Human Experience

However, working from home does not always provide a positive aspect for everyone. I mentioned earlier in this chapter that some people may suffer mental health issues like depression or isolation. Those people who live by themselves may feel isolated and wish to return to the office to be amongst their colleagues. People working from home with a family may become irritated and upset if they cannot devote the time to work or have a private space to work.

Research has shown that the idea of people panicking during a crisis is a myth (depending upon the type of crisis). In most crises, people will behave in a manner that looks after each other – the sharing and caring manner. People will take an orderly approach to a crisis.[114] People will tend to work (group) together with other affected persons, and the group's resilience grows stronger through a crisis. This same trend occurs when a crisis happens within an organisation. People will group and help each other to overcome this crisis.

Underlying questions to consider:

Why does it take a crisis before people bond together to resolve it?

Why will people not bond together for a change in the same manner as they do for a crisis?

9.3.   What COVID-19 has taught us about change

We know that change is constant and will never stop. We need to keep up with change; otherwise, we will get left behind. The change brought about by COVID-19 was unexpected and forced upon us compared to the normal changes that occur within an organisation. You can expect resistance to change during a normal organisational change, whereas the opposite occurs when there is a crisis, as illustrated in Figure 11.

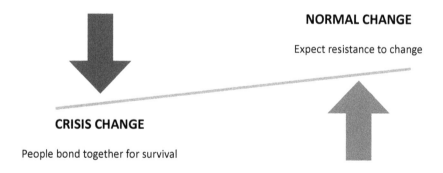

NORMAL CHANGE

Expect resistance to change

CRISIS CHANGE

People bond together for survival

Figure 11: Comparison of Change

Respected authors have gathered many thoughts to show how this pandemic has affected organisations and their people. In this section, some of these thoughts have been compiled to help understand the impacts that have been experienced and, more importantly, the lessons that we can take from this pandemic.

The COVID-19 pandemic has challenged our typical thinking about change and resistance to change.

UC Davis Health's Deputy Chief Human Resources Officer, Ekta Vyas, explains four learnings about change that we should understand.[115] She identifies the four learnings as follows:

1. Neuroscience of change has been forced to the forefront of our thinking.
2. There is a new understanding of people's resilience.
3. Changes that are not planned can lead to greater innovation.
4. Adaption and evolution are key to a sustainable pathway forward.

The impact upon segments of the organisation

Let's look at how this pandemic has influenced organisations and how we work.

Organisational change

This pandemic has disrupted economies and organisations worldwide, and to survive, companies have undergone an unprecedented transformation in their business model. The positive side to this disruptive change is that we have seen a greater will for collaboration, more innovation and improved communication, plus teams and individual employees working cohesively to enable business operations to work efficiently and effectively. [116] Before the pandemic, new changes would usually take a long time, but the pandemic has shown that change can occur within weeks.

Development of agile operations

Organisations have learned to develop more agile operations, allowing them to quickly respond to change without massive disruption.[106] Agile operations involve implementing flexible principles and methodologies into the organisation's operational processes using the available resources and will utilise human and capital resources.

One of the most significant barriers organisations have faced when adopting agile operations into their operations is their fixed cost structures. Rather than continue to use fixed cost structures, organisations can become leaner through operating variable cost structures. For example, the cost of renting commercial property for long periods has been a major barrier to moving away from a fixed cost structure. Moving to smaller premises and having a mobile hybrid workforce (on the road, working from home or coworking) removes the barrier to being cemented to a fixed cost structure.

Workforce management

The COVID-19 pandemic has also interrupted organisations concerning workforce management. Management has (and will be) suffering from the same anxieties as their employees – fear of losing their jobs, losing income, and not having the right balance of skills for the future. Managers will need to reskill and upskill themselves now to move past the pandemic and into the future.

The World Economic Forum has compiled a list of behavioural strategies to help managers reframe their approach in the future.[117] The key strategies mentioned are illustrated in Table 18.

STRATEGY	DETAIL
Employees should be treated as whole	Gone are the days when individuals were considered just for their work roles. Working from home has changed the individual to be more balanced with their personal life. Managers must accept this change and modify their mindset to accommodate for this change. Managers will need to develop holistic systems, policies, and flexible procedures for the individual and the organisation For example, some organisations recognised the strain caused to employees working from home through school holidays when their children were forced to stay at home during lockdowns. The holiday camps that would have provided some relief were not available, so some companies organised and funded children's activities during this time
Psychology safety	Managers are responsible for creating physically and mentally safe working spaces for their employees. During the work from home periods, managers should have been aware of the stress and emotional strain placed upon employees and should have reacted to the situation. Managers will need to continue their systems and processes to ensure that their employees are psychologically sound while working from home and when they return to work. The employees working from home may still be emotionally scarred, and managers will need to be aware, so they can take care of their employees. Employees' behavioural patterns have changed because of this pandemic

STRATEGY	DETAIL
Equal access to opportunities	Managers are responsible for ensuring that employees have equal access to opportunities at work whilst working from home. Managers can easily disguise or hide work opportunities when employees are not working in the office. Managers need to develop true equity to enhance equal opportunities for all employees irrespective of their gender, age, levels, background and social status

Table 18: Reframing the Approach

The workforce statistics

CIPD's research (UK) on homeworking revealed that "75% of employers expect an increased demand for homeworking" once all Government lockdowns have been lifted and businesses return to normal.[116]

Fifty-eight per cent of respondents to Omdia's Future of Work survey [118] believe that the workforce will be either hybrid or working from home as this becomes the new norm

The Omdia's Future of Work survey also revealed that 68% of enterprises saw increased productivity from employees working away from the office.

Development of agile operations

The development of agile operations will include developing agile workforce strategies and teams. Agile teams can impact a greater chance of change success as they can perform their work more effectively and efficiently, and the quality of their work becomes more premium.

Development of new skills

During the pandemic, new technologies undertaken by organisations required new skills and new roles. Some of these skills have already put pressure on workers to retrain. The workforce will need to develop new skills to retain employment in the new norm, and as organisations become more digitally enhanced and automated – otherwise, they will get left behind.

The use of freelancers

When organisations were culling employees during the early stage of the pandemic as part of their cost-cutting measures, they utilised freelancers (also known as contingent workers) for project work and to support their operating models. Freelancers are flexible, continually reskilling and upskilling themselves, and will work on projects rather than become employees of the organisation. Gartner believes that this trend will continue.[119]

Businesses will need to become digitally enhanced

The pandemic has taught organisations worldwide to become digitally enhanced, and technology has boomed. For example, forced lockdowns encouraged people to adapt to streaming TV, social media and food delivery apps. Organisations were forced to employ video conferencing to stay in contact with their employees. Technology helped employees access servers and documents via a secure environment.

Here are industry examples of how technology was used to stay in contact with customers:

- in the medical industry, telemedicine was significantly expanded to replace face-to-face interaction
- the restaurant industry was forced to use food delivery apps

Organisations should be focusing on working more in the cloud, taking advantage of automation and expanding upon-commerce.[106] Post-pandemic, organisations need to build resilient long-term strategies to minimise future business continuity risks. Long-term strategies will examine the best ways to continue to operate in the new digital enhanced world with a new talent roadmap moving forward.

Because organisations are coming to grips with the use of digital technology, employees will need to retrain and upskill to meet the change in the organisation.

Leadership

Some leaders have survived, and some have failed during the COVID-19 pandemic. What are the factors surrounding the reasons why? Rob Cross, the founder of Muru Leadership, believes leaders who are connected to the human aspect (their employees) have survived [120] and also suggests that leaders in the face of the public eye need to become more transparent with all stakeholders. Regardless of being in the public eye, leaders should be transparent in all organisations, irrespective of size.

Leaders have learnt that more emphasis needs to be placed on the workforce. Leaders in the post-pandemic are advised to continue to focus on the well-being of their workforce whilst retaining productivity levels. PwC has developed a list of six paradoxes that leaders need to move to – post-pandemic. The six paradoxes are illustrated below: [121]

1. A Localist who is globally-minded.
2. TA Politician with a high level of integrity.
3. TA Humble Hero.
4. A Strategic Executor.
5. A Humanist who is tech-savvy.
6. A Traditional Innovator.

PwC suggests those who can develop a balance between their six paradoxes will emerge as true future leaders.

9.4. The future post-COVID-19

COVID-19, in different variants, is likely here to stay; however, we will continue to adjust to and live with it: as we did with the flu. It is expected that businesses will return to pre-pandemic normalcy – but not in all situations. COVID-19 has taught us many lessons: people work differently, internal systems have been transformed from manual to automatic processes, and commercial or industrial properties have been down-sized. There is also a massive transformation to digitalisation.

Gartner has published their thoughts on future work trends and the 'new normal':[119]

1. Remote working will continue to increase.
2. Data collection on employees will be expanded to monitor employee engagement and productivity.
3. Expect to see an expansion of contingent workers.
4. Employers will continue to play a greater role in their employees' health and well-being.
5. Critical skills and roles will be separated.
6. Some employees have been dehumanised during the pandemic as employees were treated as workers first and people second.
7. There is an emergence of new employers that are classed as a top tier.
8. The design for efficiency is transitioning to the design for resilience.
9. Following the pandemic, it is expected that there will be more mergers and acquisitions with large organisations combining with other organisations or swallowing up smaller organisations that were hit by the pandemic.

As quoted by IBM – "Change remains the name of the game".[122] As organisations were forced to make significant changes to their business model, IBM points out that leaders need to think about six priorities to address in their organisations. The priorities that IBM suggest are as follows:

1. Workforce safety and security.
2. Cost management.
3. Customer retention.
4. Digital transformation.
5. Organisation agility.
6. Liquidity management.

9.5. The need for a business continuity risk management plan

A business continuity plan aims to mitigate risk and ensure recovery after a disruptive event. Yet most organisations were not prepared for the pandemic. To varying degrees, almost every company worldwide had to implement continuity actions during 2020. Deloitte's survey during the early stage of the pandemic revealed that three-quarters of the respondents had a Business Continuity Risk Management Plan (BCRMP) in place. But only 16 per cent felt their response plans worked well.[123] The question remains: why did the remaining 84 per cent of response plans not work well? The top five answers revealed in the survey:[123]

1. The response plan did not take into account pandemic specific actions.
2. Did not take into account extreme shelter-in-place.
3. Unknown how to address technology gaps.
4. The plan's foundations were solid, but the plans were not linked or harmonised.
5. There were numerous gaps in stakeholder communications.

In the same survey conducted by Deloitte, a third of firms surveyed by Deloitte created new plans on the spot through the crisis. By that time, for some organisations, this was too late.

If your organisation does not have a BCRMP, start now to develop one. If you have a BCRMP, do not let it sit in a desk drawer. The plan needs to be continually updated as risks (internal and external) are constantly changing; therefore, your plan needs to reflect new changes in risk. Equally important is evaluating and testing your BCRMP to ensure it is adequate to minimise the risk in your organisation.

Here are a few questions you should ask when creating your Business Continuity Risk Management Plan:

Does your BCRMP fulfil customer requirements?

What are the strengths and weaknesses of your Supply Chain Relationships?

Have you considered the management of employees, including their working environment plus health and safety?

How strong are your communications should a failure occur again?

Can you transition to technology?

Do you know the levels of available government support?

Do you have adequate insurance coverage?

Chapter Summary

Can your new business model survive another potential tsunami such as the COVID-19 pandemic in the future? Will you have planned workable strategies and an updated business continuity risk management plan in place should such a similar event occur?

This chapter shows traditional organisational behaviours before COVID-19 and how the pandemic turned this upside down. This pandemic has changed the way we think, the way we act and the way that we behave (leaders and employees).

The foresight of many well-respected authors has also been outlined in this chapter: suggesting how the lessons learned will change the behaviour of organisations in the future. Are you seeing these changes in your organisation?

10. Why you need digital transformation to enhance your business growth

Organisations cannot afford to miss out on digital transformation. However, too much rhetoric is placed on the word "digital" without clearly understanding how a digital presence can help organisations become better. If executed well, transforming your business model to a digitally enhanced model will help your organisation grow and prosper.

Your competitors may have or be in the process of transforming their business model to a digital model. Failure to adopt this transformation means a loss of competitive advantage, loss of newfound efficiency and loss of profits.

In this chapter, the industrial sector is used as an example to explain why they should transform their business model to a tech-enabled model and how they can benefit from maximising the impact. The end of the chapter looks at virtual communities and how they can benefit from digital transformation.

10.1. What is digitalisation?

Digitalisation

Let's start by gaining a good understanding of what is meant by "digitisation." Digitisation is the use of digital technology that removes unnecessary wastage and inefficiencies in an organisation so that the organisation can pursue value-producing opportunities. Digital technologies transfer traditional analogue information into digital information, often known as automation.

Let's showcase one area of digital technology that has helped many organisations with improved efficiency and collaboration during the COVID-19 pandemic: cloud computing. Cloud computing removes the need for in-house data storage, data losses, software updates, and daily data backups. Instead, cloud computing takes on board these activities. Xero, an accounting software program, is cloud-based, whereby users can dial into the software program providing that they have internet access. Leaders and managers have access to the latest financial information.

Advantages of digitalisation in your organisation

The key benefits digitalisation can provide your organisation [124] are:

- to disrupt your rivals with the leading-edge digital technologies to gain a competitive advantage
- to improve your business efficiencies across all sectors of the organisation
- to gain lower operating costs in all areas of your organisation
- to reduce human errors
- to support better data analysis
- to provide better collaboration if digitalisation involves using the cloud
- to provide automation of mundane tasks
- to bring your products faster to market

- to provide greater data security, automatic updates and backing up of data
- to provide the opportunity to bring new innovative ideas to your organisation.

Digital transformation

To go one step further, what do we mean when using the term "digital transformation"? The transformation to digital requires a change in the organisation's strategies, plus the mindset and beliefs of leaders and managers to influence change through digital technologies. The transformation occurs when applying digital technologies to all sectors of an organisation.[125] The transformation will impact business processes, activities and competencies. Digital transformation improves and provides new capabilities to create customer value and faster response to market changes and economic conditions.

Apart from the transformation to digital technologies, Vitaliy Zhovtyuk, a Systems Architect and Technical Leader, states that the discipline of change management within an organisation needs to change in line with the changes in digital technology to meet the newer challenges that need to be faced. He describes that the process of change management will need to consider the effects on human behaviour and user experience from the transformation to digital technology.[126] Previously, digital technology was introduced first, followed by modifications to change management. This philosophy has to be reversed: modifications to change management must be considered *before* the changes in digital technology. One of the key elements of the bringing forth of change management is the consideration of the organisation's culture. The culture will change due to changes in digital transformation. Leaders and managers must adopt empathy as empathy will build trust.[127]

Before the leaders and managers of an organisation rush into the digital technology era, it must have a clear vision of its objectives.[127] The leaders and managers must develop strong digital strategies and align them with the overall objectives to see if they make sense.

10.2. Digital impact on organisations

Digital transformation will be forever ongoing. New inventions, new ideas, new processes and new activities will be created through digital technology. The COVID-19 pandemic has shown how organisations were forced to respond to digital transformation within weeks and months. Previously it would have taken years to complete the transformation. The team at IT Pro is quoted as saying that *"technology is not a choice, but a fundamental business strategy that must be interwoven into every part of an organisation"*.[128]

Leaders and managers are also demanding solutions that are available on-demand through agile hybrid IT services and agile networking capabilities. These same people are looking at the existing manual processes and seeking alternate ways to automate them. In some organisations, payroll functions and some accounting functions are still performed by manual methods. Automating these functions will help employees become more productive, and managers can focus on better opportunities for the organisation.

Reasons why you cannot do without digital transformation

On the next page I list some of the most important reasons your organisation cannot do without digital transformation.[124][128]

IMPACT	DETAILS
Your customers' buying habits have changed	Due to their busy personal and work lifestyles, customers find it easier and more convenient to shop online. Their buying habits were changing before COVID-19 but were reinforced during lockdowns. Online shopping has brought convenience to customers wishing to shop any time of day or night and from anywhere. This change in buying habits has extended further to customers comparing your products and your competitors' products (Factory Dev, n.d.). Your organisation needs to find these customers again Another change in customer habits is that customers are seeking products or services that are readily on demand
Digitalisation is cheaper	Digitalisation provides lower operating costs
Communication channels are extended	The use of digital channels is used more widely. Channels include social media, emails, websites and mobile applications. You can also consider setting up an omnichannel strategy if it applies to your industry
Innovation can be created	Digitalisation provides automation that frees up time for employees, thus allowing them to become more innovative and creative with ideas, activities and processes
Maximise customer journey and experience	Make the customer's journey fun and exciting throughout the entire process. Digital technology will help improve the customer's experience

IMPACT	DETAILS
Don't forget about mobile phone users	As people are moving away from computers and increasing their usage of mobile phones, there must be strategies in place to entice mobile phone users
Consider the benefits to employees	Employees enjoy the benefits of using digital technologies, providing they can understand the benefits to themselves
Data security	Data security poses new and additional risks when transforming to digital technologies. The global lockdowns presented greater risk challenges for IT professionals. People were forced to work from home, thus exposing greater risk to illegal access to data. IT professionals have performed a magnificent job in securing data under such challenging conditions
Strengthening business partnerships	Business partnerships throughout the supply chain are critical to the success of all organisations. Existing partnerships can be strengthened further by streamlining the processes and activities through digital technologies

Table 19: The reasons why your organisation needs digital transformation

Transforming an organisation's change from aspiration to reality has become possible through a digital transformation, but it needs employees who have the skills and experience to use these digital tools.

Gartner is further quoted as saying that *"A Lack of Digital Business Competence Will Cause 25 Percent of Businesses to Lose Competitive Ranking by 2017"*.[129] As far back as 2014, digital was becoming a new trend for organisations worldwide. At that time, Gartner pointed out that six steps should be considered when thinking about transforming your business to digital. These steps are still relevant today:[129]

STEP	REQUIREMENT
1	The mindset has to be right, and there must be a shared understanding
2	The organisation must have the right leaders in place
3	A Digital Business Centre of Excellence is needed in the organisation
4	Formulation of a digital strategy to take advantage of opportunities and respond to risks
5	Digital Business Skills and Roles are needed to master the new digital technologies
6	The new digital business must be able to create capabilities

Table 20: Gartner's six steps to digital transformation

Predictions and trends in the marketplace

According to ZDNet, the digital transformation industry is expected to continue growing. The projections put forth by ZDNet reveal that investment in digital transformation will be over $6.8 trillion between 2020 and 2023, and it is expected that the digital transformation market will experience a compound annual growth rate (CAGR) of 15.5%.[130]

In 2021 we saw significant shifts taking place due to the pandemic. For example, the move to hybrid working, an increase in Ransomware attacks across the world and the adoption of Microsoft Teams to keep communication channels open and keep everyone connected.

Blue Car Technologies Limited and [x]cube LABS foresee the following digital and digital transformation trends [131] [132] happening in 2022:

- there will be an increase in process automation
- AI and Machine Learning will continue to rise
- The Bring-Your-Own-Device (BYOD) program is expected to enjoy widespread adoption
- the security feature of Multi-factor Authentication will be used more frequently to replace passwords
- the continued rise of cloud-based phone systems
- the placement of greater emphasis on security and privacy
- an increase in the workload in the cloud will also become innovative
- zero Trust Principles will become more widely adopted
- the adoption of 5G
- greater use of the Metaverse
- instead of just the SAAS model, Everything-As-A-Service (EAAS) will become more widely accepted
- greater use of NFTs.

Review the list of the above trends and see which can benefit your organisation.

10.3. Why industrials should pursue a tech-enabled transformation

The industrial sector is recognised as a capital-intensive industry and relies heavily upon research and development to draw upon innovations and technologies. However, the investment in capital assets can quickly become obsolete if new capital assets with further features and technologies are made available soon after.

If industrial organisations do not shift to the tech-enabled transformation now, they will be left behind as market and economic dynamics forever shift. Competitiveness increases as existing and new competitors with new technologies enter the market.[133] Industrial organisations will need to keep reinvesting in new capital assets or update their existing assets with the latest technology.

An industrial organisation's failure to take on tech-enabled technology will give its competitors a leading edge. Organisation and brand equity diminish when competitors produce products faster, more efficiently and at a lower cost, thus driving the market price downwards: by simply using new technologies, those competitors will use the latest tech-enabled technologies to disrupt the marketplace.

According to McKinsey, leaders of industrial and manufacturing organisations using machine-intelligence technologies achieve three to four times greater improvement impact. Figure 12 illustrates how organisations have benefited from machine intelligence.[134]

Average improvement through machine intelligence, by KPI, %

● Bottom 50% ◦ Top quartile

Category	KPI
Efficiency	Factory
	Labor
	Equipment
Cost	Operating cost
	Warehousing
	Quality
	Inventory
	Product cost
Revenue	Revenue
	Demand accuracy
Responsiveness	Lead time
	Speed to market
	Design time
	Lot size
	Changeovers
Customer experience	Service
	Net promoter score
	Complaints
Environmental	Environmental impact
	Energy efficiency
	Employee satisfaction

Figure 12: Machine intelligence improvements (Source – https://www.mckinsey.com/ business-functions/risk-and-resilience/our-insights/covid-19-implications-for-business)

An industrial organisation that transforms to tech-enabled technologies will enjoy the benefits of improved productivity, additional revenues and revenue streams, plus increased profits and cash flows.

10.4. How to maximise the impact of tech-enabled transformations

Before COVID-19, digital transformation was based on automating manual activities and processes proposed and implemented by the senior IT executive. Today, digital transformation is more than just automation and is now controlled by leaders and managers.

McKinsey states three factors are reshaping the industrial sector, and leaders should think about them now. The industrial sector is seeing the dynamic shifting with (i) the workforce, (ii) customer and supplier ecosystems moving faster and (iii) digital disrupters.[133]

Let's look at ways to maximise the impact of tech-enabled transformations in your industrial organisation.

Industrial organisations should become more proactive with business intelligence analytics to understand better their suppliers' and customers' behaviours and habits. Industrial organisations will need self-service data prep and analytics tools to improve collaboration. According to Devpro, the business intelligence market is expected to grow to $30.9 billion this year.[135]

Leaders and managers of industrial organisations must change their present mindset to a cloud-first mentality for business analytics. Adopting a cloud-first mentality will cover core business applications such as human resource management systems, supply chain management, customer relationship management and enterprise resource planning. There may also be other lines of business that can be transferred to the cloud.

Expect to see more mergers and acquisitions in 2022. Many industrial organisations have excelled during the COVID-19 pandemic by changing their business models, including human and capital resources, collaboration, supply chain management and building better customer relationships. However, not all industrial organisations enjoyed the same success. These industrial organisations may be merged or acquired with those industrial organisations that performed with excellence.

Now is the time to rebalance the organisation's culture as it will have been severely disrupted during the pandemic. Employees were forced into lockdowns, meaning they had to work differently, leading to new emotions and behaviours. Managers will (or can expect to) experience these different behaviours and emotions on their employees' return to the workplace, and these emotions and behaviours will ultimately change the organisation's culture.

Your industrial organisation needs to build a resilient, environmentally friendly business model that reduces the impact of climate change [136]. However, the adoption of digital transformation across multiple sectors will provide greater collaboration. The World Economic Forum reports that the Information and Communications Technology sector produces 1.4% of global greenhouse gases. This sector has the capability of cutting these emissions by 15% across other industry sectors. It is reported that the 5G network will further cut emissions by using renewable energy options, smarter power grids that support electric vehicles and smart manufacturing. Other areas that can help reduce the impact of climate change are artificial intelligence and IoT.

Your industrial organisation requires a long-term sustainable business model that needs to be robust, flexible and resilient to withstand shifts in the market and economic dynamics.

10.5. Challenges associated with tech-enabled transformations

Adopting tech-enabled transformation will improve your organisation's efficiencies, productivity, and finances. However, although tech-enabled change might seem optimistic, there are also challenges. AI Multiple [137] identifies five challenges that apply to all organisations, not just industrial. The challenges include:

1. A shortage of talent. Does your organisation have the best leaders, managers and employees that have the digital and technical skills to use the tech-enabled technologies?

2. Resistance to the transformation. Organisations must expect some employees to resist the change due to fear of losing their jobs. It is up to the managers to foster a change management culture that communicates the importance and benefits of tech-enabled transformation.
3. Tech-enabled transformation leads to greater security risks. The greater spread of technology throughout the organisation and employees working remotely increases the risk of data leakage, Ransomware and potentially exposed areas of vulnerabilities for hackers. Leaders and managers need to develop strong cybersecurity procedures in-house or outsource to suppliers. They need to identify vulnerabilities in their system.
4. Agile transformation. The most common challenges with developing agile transformation in your organisation include (i) inconsistent practices and processes across all divisions, (ii) resistance to change and (iii) agile values are not aligned with the organisation's culture.
5. Not enough funds available. Organisations have been bleeding from the fast erosion of cash flow during the pandemic spent on unplanned investments in technology. The erosion of cash flow was important to keep organisations and their employees safe during the pandemic. Organisations will have more time now to properly plan their next transformations and ensure that they have cash flow on hand (or are capable of raising) before investing.

10.6. Best practices for digital transformation

Digital transformation can be successfully implemented and adopted by your stakeholders simply by applying best practices.[138] Below are some best practices you can employ within your organisation:

UNDERSTAND THE BUSINESS PROBLEM. What is the business problem that needs to be solved? Production optimisation, customer satisfaction, sustainability? If the problem exists with the customers or users, managers need to understand the situation from their perspective. Once the problem has been understood, you can define the user requirements and determine the best practice to solve the problem

ENCOURAGE TEAM COLLABORATION. Prioritise the collaboration needed by teams as each team has a different skill set and practices required to achieve the organisation's objectives.

The organisation's culture must be flexible enough to allow change to occur.

HAVE A CORPORATE GOVERNANCE POLICY IN PLACE. Remember that it will need to be regularly updated as changes occur.

BE AWARE OF SUNKEN COSTS. These are often incurred by replacing existing technologies with newer ones. Technology has a legacy cost.

10.7. What to expect with new digital marketing trends

Krista Neher, best-selling author, international speaker and CEO of Boot Camp Digital, has provided insight into the trends likely to occur in digital marketing in 2022.[139] Those insights include:

1. Metaverse will become universal in providing augmented and virtual experiences. Organisations can utilise the metaverse to deliver these experiences to their stakeholders.
2. As more organisations move to digital marketing, this will prompt growth in jobs for digital marketing.
3. The use of influencer marketing is expected to continue to grow. Customers love product or service endorsements from influencers.
4. Privacy regulations will hinder the opportunity for marketers to use data captured in artificial intelligence.
5. More and more organisations are using LinkedIn to extend their reach to customers, suppliers and employees.
6. Websites should be fully mobile optimised for smartphone users.
7. Algorithms are driving digital marketing experiences through social media.
8. Creating experiences for their customers. New experiences are needed throughout every interaction of your customers' journey.

10.8. Virtual communities in a virtual world

Before COVID-19, behaviour change management concentrated on real-world organisations. Now that organisations transfer their operations digitally, virtual communities and worlds have emerged and remained dominant post-pandemic. Therefore, behaviour change management will continue to focus on real-world organisations that have not transitioned to digitalisation plus address virtual communities and the world.

Each segment of the virtual community will have different values, behaviours and habits which may significantly differ from those in the real world. Therefore, the virtual world's values, behaviours and habits will need to be tempered and aligned with the organisation's values and objectives. Consideration must be given to the work/life balance that has been extended in the virtual world. Employees working from home have had to balance their personal life and work.

Chapter Summary

It is crucial that when an organisation undergoes a digital transformation (small or large), the developed digital strategies must align with the organisation's objectives. The digital transformation must increase efficiencies and productivity, reduce operational costs, and increase revenues and business opportunities. The digital transformation change needs to be adequately planned, communicated and executed by the managers and employees.

Communication of the change to digital technology to employees must be done at the early stage of planning so that managers can identify resistance to the change and take care of any resistance at the beginning of the process. Those employees that have accepted the concept of digital transformation can feel part of the process. Employees can take ownership of their role in the digital transformation.

11. The impact of artificial intelligence on human behaviour

Artificial intelligence (AI) is a disruptive technology that impacts organisations worldwide: shaping organisations and human behaviour – whether we like it or not. Humans have been interacting with machines for many years: on the production line or simply using a computer. Organisations that recognise and adopt this change can take advantage of AI to gain more customers, improve efficiencies plus gain a competitive advantage over their rivals.

This chapter starts with a clear definition of artificial intelligence. It then outlines how AI can benefit your organisation, how it can impact human behaviour and explains what you can do to manage human behaviour.

11.1. What is artificial intelligence?

Artificial intelligence uses machines that display intelligence similar to humans.[140] However, it also differs from human intelligence. Organisations require any or all three types of AI (i) business processes to be automated, (ii) improving the experience with employees and customers, plus (iii) gaining a better insight into data analytics.[141] Artificial intelligence is not a system by itself as it is incorporated into a system. Artificial intelligence occurs when a machine can perform tasks without any supervision or input from a human. That is, the machine is capable of visual perception, recognition of speech and making its own decisions. Therefore, the machine must be capable of learning, logically reasoning, and self-correcting itself if it causes an error.

IBM nicely summarises the definition of artificial intelligence as follows:

> **"Artificial intelligence leverages computers and machines to mimic the problem-solving and decision-making capabilities of the human mind."**
>
> *IBM Cloud Education* [142]

Artificial intelligence can be broken down into four goals (refer to Table 21) that ultimately link to AI's definition. Authors of Artificial Intelligence: A Modern Approach, Russell and Norvig [143] suggest that artificial intelligence aims to achieve four goals:[142]

THE HUMAN APPROACH	THE IDEAL APPROACH
Machines that can act like humans	Machines that can act rationally
Machines that can think like humans	Machines that can think rationally

Table 21: Deeper understanding of defining artificial intelligence

11.2. How AI is already implemented in organisations

Artificial intelligence allows machines to perform tasks in a human-like manner simply from learning from experience. Machines can learn and adjust to new data through deep learning that will enable them to process large volumes of data and perform specific tasks mimicking a human-like approach.

Organisations are already using artificial intelligence by adopting smart technology to help improve business functions and improve the customers' experience.

Let's take a deeper look at how some organisations are adopting AI into their business.[144][145]

Information Management Systems. Organisations will use artificial intelligence when scanning or uploading documents onto their platforms. The platform will scan the document to determine its type (invoice, correspondence, agreements etc.) and file the document into the appropriate filing system on the platform.

Processes and Workflows become automated. AI is used to eliminate mundane manual processes by automating these processes. It is often used to eliminate manual data entry and re-entering of data. Workflows can become automated once the processes have been automated using artificial intelligence. The following examples demonstrate how:

EXAMPLE ONE. If your organisation provides a continual monthly service to a customer, AI intelligence will automate the invoice process by repeatedly preparing the invoice (normally monthly) without human intervention.

EXAMPLE TWO. Some cloud-based accounting software programs will allow you to simplify your bank account reconciliations. If you have repeating bank entries such as bank fees, you can create a bank rule rather than keep entering the details manually each time these bank entries occur. The bank rule will allow you to automatically set the conditions and instructions for when this type of bank entry occurs.

Tightening security and governance controls. AI is used in many ways across all industry sectors and, in particular, to detect and prevent fraudulent activities and restrict access to information and automate records management.

Improve the customer experience. Chatbots, also known as virtual assistants, appear on websites and mobile applications designed to help customers find products or resolve queries they may have about a product. Chatbots will direct the customer to where they want to go quicker, thus saving the customer time.

In the future, the use of **conversational artificial intelligence** will be used by many organisations to provide a more personalised customer experience. The conversational artificial intelligence will become almost human-like with speech-based virtual assistants that will guide the customer to find the product or service or resolve any other query.

Number crunching. AI will be used more frequently to perform number-crunching tasks and big data analytics. Artificial intelligence in this scenario will free employees' time to concentrate on analysis and decision making.

Questions to consider...

How is your organisation using AI currently?

How can AI add benefit to your organisation?

11.3. Benefits of artificial intelligence

Artificial intelligence will benefit organisations across all industry sectors: let's take a moment to look at how. Reference is made to Table 22. [140] [146][147][148]

NO	KEY BENEFIT	DETAILS
1	Your organisation can save time and money by using AI	Repetitive tasks can be optimised and performed accurately. Machines can replace mundane tasks, which allow humans to perform more productive tasks
2	Customer interactions are automated	Interaction with customers is best suited with a human touch. However, machines are slowly learning the process of developing the human touch. For example, chatbots can initiate conversations when a human visits a website or mobile app
3	The customer experience can be improved	Machine Learning will study each customer's history and behaviour and give your operator better ways to handle each customer. A classic example is shopping websites that provide you with alternative or similar ideas. For instance, ordering a pair of shoes. The artificial intelligence will offer suggestions for similar style shoes to those you have looked at previously. If you are a frequent visitor to a shopping website, AI will also provide a listing of previous purchases as a reminder
4	Predicts outcomes based upon the data	Machines can provide a better prediction of outcomes based on the available data. It is useful in solving complex problems. Article intelligence can predict customer behaviour based on the customer's previous buying history

NO	KEY BENEFIT	DETAILS
5	Reduce human error	Typically, people will make mistakes. These mistakes can occur for many reasons; for example, they may be suffering from personal or work-related stress. Artificial intelligence will reduce the possibility of human errors simply by automating manual processes and tasks.
6	Improving employee efficiency and productivity	The automation of business processes and workflows will reduce the workload burden on the employee. It will increase employee productivity as more time can be spent on more productive areas of the business
7	Reduce labour-intensive industries	Labour-intensive organisations can improve productivity through the use of AI. For example, Amazon employs AI-enabled robots in their warehouses, which takes out the labour intensity of fulfilment
8	Predicting natural disasters	AI uses recognition algorithms to pre-empt the likelihood of natural disasters so that organisations can prepare themselves
9	Business continuity	Risk analysis and management are critical for an organisation's survival. The COVID-19 pandemic showed the strengths of those organisations with a risk management plan in place. The pandemic also revealed the weaknesses of organisations without a risk management plan. Artificial intelligence will help leaders and managers plan risk management strategies and respond to any crisis faster

Table 22: Key Benefits of using Artificial Intelligence

11.4. Artificial intelligence – is it bad news?

No. Artificial intelligence is not bad news. Using artificial intelligence will help improve efficiencies, productivity, employee and customer relationships, and financial performance.

There may be limitations to how AI can currently work best in your organisation. Still, it's likely the benefits of adopting AI far outweigh the limitations you are presently experiencing. Additionally, it is expected that the limitations are only short-term until new developments take place to reduce the limitations.

Conversely, AI can be ineffective across many areas of your organisation too. Let's look at some areas artificial intelligence will **not** help your organisation [146] – perhaps debunking the myths and the theories that robots and machines will take over the world!

1. Machines cannot program themselves; they need human intervention to instruct them on what they have to do.
2. AI cannot create content without guidelines. Therefore, employees need to give instructions
3. AI cannot invent, be innovative or develop new ideas at this stage.
4. AI cannot make ethical decisions because it does not experience emotions and feelings. Although it can make decisions, it needs a human perspective to see if they are ethically correct.

For decades, scaremongering regarding AI taking over the world has been rife: often caused by the misunderstanding and misinterpretation of information. When the first computer was introduced, the fear was that the computer might exceed human intelligence. There were other fears that computers might take over learning, reasoning and complex decision-making. Consequently, people feared that computers would replace people.[149] The concept of "smart systems" provided more fear, particularly with employees losing their jobs.

The latest scaremongering is that robots will take over the world by developing superintelligence. Superintelligence is intelligence that surpasses human intelligence.[150] Do you think robots and machines can develop intelligent behaviour superior to human intelligence? In my opinion, this fear will be short-lived as people will come to see the benefits they can obtain from artificial intelligence.

However, what must be considered is that wealth inequality is likely to widen. As the wealthier people get rich and the poorer people head towards poverty [151], the more affluent people will reap the benefits from their investment in artificially based technologies and from organisations that have undertaken artificial intelligence. The poorer people will suffer from the loss of employment and loss of income.

11.5. How humans should and will adapt to artificial intelligence

Impact on employees

For leaders and managers, AI is exciting, and you should progress further with implementing it into your organisation. However, we must not forget how artificial intelligence will impact human resources within an organisation. Inevitably, artificial intelligence will make *some* jobs across all industries redundant. If there are massive redundancies worldwide, consideration needs to be given to the lack of upskilling and the social upheavals that could occur.

Employees will need to upskill themselves to learn more about artificial intelligence to avoid being made redundant. They will need to know more about the science of AI and how to use its analytical skills. Employees will need to understand, interpret, analyse and make decisions arising from the outputs of machine learning and advanced analytics.[145] If the employees are not capable of being upskilled and cannot be allocated to other areas within your organisation, then these employees will be without a job.

Changing processes through streamlining may lead to employee resistance. Employees will resist change if there is fear that they will lose their job; therefore, communication with employees is essential from the beginning to the end of the change. Communication will involve outlining the complete process of the change plus the impact and benefits for employees. You will need to *engage* the employees in the change process.

Artificial intelligence will also be used to improve human relationships. In the future, relationship bots will be used to predict the success of human relationships and assess other human qualities and their level of trustworthiness.

The role of the human resource department

It is predicted that the Human Resource department will play more of an administrative role as AI will play a more significant role in selecting the best candidates for job roles.[145] A concern is that artificial intelligence may choose the wrong candidate if the input data is incorrect, so arguably, some elements of the traditional role of the human resources department should not be left to AI decision making. Human interaction with potential candidates is still needed to help identify the best person(s) for the role. However, artificial intelligence can be used to eliminate the mundane task of searching through hundreds or even thousands of job applications. There's no doubt AI will soon play a significant role in deciding if a person successfully gets the job.

The possibility of employees working together with artificial intelligence

Can an employee work together with AI? The simple answer is YES. Employees have already been working together with artificial intelligence to date. Artificial intelligence has not reduced employee capabilities but has augmented their capabilities. Despite resistance from employees whose roles machines have replaced, this trend will continue in the future, and AI will continue to disrupt how organisations operate and how employees will perform their tasks and activities.

Employees and AI can work together through collaboration. Leaders and managers need to have the appropriate strategies to provide a supportive relationship between employees and machines. That may seem a strange statement – but two-way collaboration is necessary between machines and employees. They need to obtain the best from the machines whilst improving business processes and optimising how humans can best work together with artificial intelligence machines to achieve maximum efficiencies.[152]

To enhance this collaboration, employees must undertake three roles.[152]

1. The first role is for employees to train the machines to perform tasks. The machine-learning algorithms must be given instructions and be trained on how they are to perform tasks.
2. The second role is to explain the outcomes arising from the output from the machines. The machines will undertake tasks or perform big data analysis to provide an output. Artificial intelligence cannot explain the outcome, and only employee intervention can explain the results.
3. The third role is to make machines sustainable. Organisations will need employees who can ensure that the machines are working correctly, responsibly, and safely.

At the same time, machines can be used to assist employees in expanding their capabilities in performing their tasks. Likewise, machines can undertake three roles in helping employees.[152]

1. Machines can increase employees' cognitive strengths. Artificial intelligence can improve an employee's level of creativity and analytic and decision-making abilities.
2. Machines can interact with employees and customers. Employees can enjoy more free time as machines perform tasks on their behalf so that employees can spend more time on productive tasks. Machines can interact with customers through chatbots, thus improving their experience with the organisation.
3. Machines can improve and embody an employee's physical and mental capabilities.

Pew Research Centre [149] puts forth a list of concerns that experts have raised regarding the impact of artificial intelligence and the future of people:

- humans fear that they will lose control over their life
- humans fear that they will lose their jobs because an organisation has taken on artificial intelligence, which could result in greater social upheavals
- humans fear that artificial intelligence can abuse their personal information
- humans fear the potential increase in cybercrime.

We can already see how artificial intelligence plays a part in our lives today. It is not only impacting adults but children too. Our social interactions are already intertwined with digital transformation and AI, and these social interactions will develop further in the future. Digital transformation and artificial intelligence will be with us for a long time!

Chapter Summary

Artificial intelligence offers multiple benefits to organisations, but there are downsides.

Organisations can improve their financial performance, increase efficiencies and productivity, and gain a competitive advantage over their rivals using artificial intelligence.

Leaders and managers must be aware of the pitfalls of AI that can occur with their most-prized asset – employees. Planning and communication are the key strategies that need to be employed to transition from existing processes to new ones successfully.

12. Monitoring change

Why is it important to monitor the change within your organisation?

Let's demonstrate the impact of monitoring or not monitoring a change within an organisation by example: a change in accounting software.

The plan to change the accounting software from X to Y might be perfectly planned with all contingencies and risks considered. If the change is properly managed throughout the process, risks will be minimised, checklists ticked off, and financial account balances and statements will be correct.

However, if the change is not monitored, there is a good chance that the financial account balances will *not* be accurate. Errors can occur without being identified during the process of changing the accounting software, and future financial statements will be incorrect, thus presenting false financial performance and position statements.

This chapter explains the importance of monitoring and measuring the effect of change. The use of CMO (Change Management Office) and PMO (Project Management Office) strategies will help guide you to which strategies are best for your next planned change. Unfortunately, COVID-19 forced change upon all organisations for survival. Little time was spent on understanding the CMO and PMO strategies. This chapter also reinforces how and why these strategies can benefit your organisation.

12.1. The revolutionisation of change management

Change management started to emerge over 25 years ago, even though the concept of change occurred in Ancient Greek times.[153] Change management began to take meaningful form pre-1990 when the underlying concept of human experience changes was understood.[8] During the 1990s, businesses became aware of change management even though the practice was still misunderstood. In 2000, change management became formalised with more resources and tools. Leaders and managers started to develop job positions for change management in their organisations. They became more conscious of the psychological aspects and social impact of human behaviour. Today, change management has evolved into a recognised discipline. The move towards automation, digital technology, and artificial intelligence has forced leaders and managers to think and react more deeply to the human experience change. The leaders and managers of today are now focused on sustainability and the impact of their organisation on the world.

12.2. How to measure change and why it is important

Importance of measuring change

Although measuring change is vital to the ultimate success of the change or project, managers have often failed to include a measurement strategy in their change management framework. The measurement strategy is often excluded from this important strategy because of the lack of knowledge and understanding and because it is considered complicated. Prosci identifies the following areas of change management or project that managers should measure:[154]

- organisational performance
- individual performance
- change management performance
- effectiveness of change management activities
- achievement and benefits arising from outcomes.

What is being measured during the change?

It is essential to know what is being measured during the change. Collin Andrews, MBA and project manager at Printpack, refers to the two types of measurements useful during a change management process [155] as (i) qualitative and (ii) quantitative.

Qualitative measurement is not quantitative; it cannot be measured by numbers but by judgment or a statement. However, some of the qualitative judgements can be supported by quantitative factors. For example, a person may not be working to their full potential today. This statement is a qualitative statement that in itself may be difficult to measure and support. However, there may be many quantitative factors that will back up the qualitative statement.

Using the previous example, it is easy to assume that the qualitative statement may be challenging to measure. But it can be measured by establishing qualitative factors that become the criteria for measurement. The qualitative factors become the checklist that will be measured to see if the factors have been achieved or not.

Quantitative measurement is something that can be easily measured through a metric. The metric must be aligned with the objectives for the change management. For example, a metric might be to reduce operational costs by 20% within three months after the change management process has been implemented. This metric is measurable. The downside to using metrics for measurement is that it is backwards looking – it looks at historical information to provide the measurement. The previous data may not be representative of current or future data. The current and future data may present a different outlook perspective that needs to be considered.

If we break the measurement down even further, five key areas should be measured, including (i) scheduling, (ii) quality, (iii) cost implications, (iv) performance and (v) stakeholder satisfaction.[156]

Another perspective on measurement

The scheduling area is the project plan and the stages required to reach the end of the project. Each project will have different stages that must be reached before starting the next. Measuring the progress of each phase ensures that the outcomes of that stage have been reached and that the timing and costs fall within budget.

Quality assurance should be undertaken at the end of each stage of the project. The quality assurance process should review the quality of the change management process and identify areas that could need improvement.

Each project or change management should have a detailed budget outlining the costs likely to be incurred. The budget should be broken by costs for each milestone to be attained. The actual costs should be measured against its retrospective budget. If the actual costs for any of the milestones attained are over budget, analysis and explanation will be needed to understand the cause of the overspend.

After each milestone, a measurement of the benefits and performance attained should be undertaken. The measurements should be analysed to see if there will be a material impact on the change or project result.

In most cases, the stakeholder is the employee assisting with the project or change management. The measurement of their performance and satisfaction should be undertaken throughout the change to highlight any areas of difficulties and non-satisfaction. Leaders and managers can quickly react to any difficulties or non-satisfaction before the next milestone is attained.

A third perspective

The Switzerland-based International Labour Organization states that outcomes need to be measured against targets. They suggest that targets should be *"particular values specified for an indicator to be accomplished in a specific timeframe"*.[157] Their definition of a metric is similar to the definitions mentioned previously – but with a marginal difference. The marginal difference is that their definition includes the words *"specific timeframe."* The suggested use of a timeframe within the metric or target is to avoid the objective not being reached. Targets or metrics must be time-specific.

The importance of analysing the measurement outcome

It is crucial to analyse the outcome of the metric measurement as there may be underlying problems within the organisation.[155] It is best to show the possible issues that could occur if the metric measurement was favourable.

Example

Using the previous example: reduce operational costs by 20% (metric) within three months (time-specific) after implementing the change management process. Let's assume it is now three months later. The metric measurement shows that the organisation has reduced operational expenses by 22% within the three months. On the surface of it, the outcome that has been achieved is awesome. The organisation has excelled at the objective by an extra 10% saving in operational costs. The metric needs to be analysed to determine any underlying problems.

Continuing with the example above, two underlying problems were discovered during the outcome analysis. The first underlying problem was that fifty per cent of the sales employees had left the organisation. The second underlying problem was that sales were down by 40% due to fewer sales employees.

Conclusion. Even though the overall objective was achieved, and the organisation can feel proud of achieving that metric, it is important to analyse the metric measurement as it could lead to underlying problems elsewhere within the organisation.

12.3. What is a Change Management Office?

A Change Management Office (CMO) is usually a separate department within an organisation that plans the strategy, processes, objectives and implementation of change management. The Change Management Office becomes the focal point for oversight, planning, decision-making, implementing, measurement and making change sustainable.[158]

The type and size of a CMO will vary in each organisation depending upon the needs and complexity of the change. Prosci's research found that in most organisations that had implemented a CMO, the team had between two to five people regardless of the organisation's size.[159] The size of the CMO does not matter, providing the team is strong enough to plan and implement change. Sometimes, the size of the CMO team will need to be increased, subject to the size of the change.

In research conducted by Prosci, it was found that the Change Management Office was going to be the number two trend in the change management discipline in future years.[159]

A common issue found in a CMO was that the people working within the CMO often found it frustrating due to the lack of clarity of what the stakeholders need and unstable demand. These frustrations can be overcome quickly through strong leadership, management and communication.

Why is CMO needed?

As a single point of contact within an organisation, a CMO can become more effective at transforming and executing a change. The team led by experienced managers will have had sufficient experience in change management to overcome barriers to resistance and other impediments to change. The team within the CMO will be able to manage the change quickly. Based on the team's skills and experience, they will be proactive and foresee likely impediments, resolving them before they occur.

Any organisation can set up a CMO regardless of size and industry sector. Whilst considering the requirements for your own CMO, there are three elements that you will need to consider.

ELEMENT ONE. Defining the purpose of the CMO. You need to establish the guidelines for the CMO. Prosci's survey revealed the most common responsibilities of a CMO included owning and maintaining the Change Management methodology and its corresponding tools. The survey also revealed that it was the responsibility of the CMO to provide support to project teams plus offer all of the necessary resources to handle specific projects.

Who will be the leader of the CMO? The leader will be designated with specific responsibilities that need to be accomplished. The leader will need to define the size of the CMO, determining the number of employees and the role they will play in the CMO.

ELEMENT TWO. Type of CMO. What kind of CMO should be implemented in your organisation? There are typically three types to consider (i) hybrid, (ii) centralised or (iii) decentralised. No type is deemed correct – choose what will be best for your organisation's culture.

ELEMENT THREE. Where does the CMO fit in your organisation? This is a common question! The fitting of the CMO within your organisation will depend upon the answers to the two elements mentioned above.

The services provided by a CMO

The CMO will provide the following services within an organisation:

- change management methodology
- planning
- communication across all areas of the change management
- toolkits including checklists and templates
- implementation guidelines
- measuring metrics
- reporting on the progress of change implementation
- lessons to be learned
- training programs for employees
- training programs for the CMO team.

Value-adding

Does a Change Management Office add value to an organisation? According to Issoria, the common belief amongst the executives surveyed was that the Change Management Office did offer value to an organisation.[160]

Here are what some of the experts are saying about the value of CMO:

> "A strong CMO will ensure that change management is executed most appropriately and effectively. This in turn will result in changes being delivered effectively and efficiently, and outcomes and benefits are fully achieved. The CMO should result in a faster path to benefits realization, and better sustainment of those benefits."
>
> *Richard Newton, a non-executive director at Issoria* [160]

Let's look at how some CMOs can benefit your organisation:[159][158]

- changes that are delivered efficiently and effectively
- a single point of contact for managing the change
- the right leaders are in place to manage the change
- the team is experienced, so they will not be stressed
- cost of change management should be lower
- a better understanding of human and capital resources needed for the change
- external partners should be used during peak change periods
- culture will be improved through strong change management processes
- outcomes are achieved faster
- outcomes will be more sustainable through new processes, technology and infrastructure
- a CMO creates credibility within and outside of the organisation.

12.4. The benefits of a Project Management Office

What is a Project Management Office?

A Project Management Office (PMO) is a focal point within an organisation that manages projects and can best be described as a team, group or department of an organisation, depending upon the need or size of the PMO. The use of PMOs has become more prevalent within organisations.

Research undertaken by PM Solutions found that organisations with a dedicated PMO increased from 48% in 2000 to 85% in 2016.[161]

The Project Management Office serves a similar purpose to the CMO regarding managing a project from start to finish: coordinating the planning and implementation of projects. The team will establish the processes, standards, best practices, training and key metrics needed to complete projects.[161]

Why is PMO needed?

A PMO is needed in your organisation if you are finding the following failures with deliveries of projects (or change):

- projects are not meeting the deadlines
- project costs are exceeding the budget
- project outcomes are not being achieved
- projects are not sustainable
- inconsistent workflows between like-minded projects
- projects do not follow best practices.

Development of a PMO

Does your organisation need a PMO? Forethought needs to be considered when deciding whether your organisation needs to have a PMO. There are typically three types of PMO that can be formed in an organisation (i) supportive, (ii) controlling and (iii) directive.[162]

A **supportive PMO** is used to influence rather than be directive or controlling. The people within a supportive PMO will be advisors rather than having any authority to direct an employee to take action. A **controlling PMO** means that the team have the power to implement best practices plus control activities and compliance. A **directive PMO** takes control of the project. This type of PMO is not supportive or controlling.

Figure 13 illustrates a typical (but not definitive) PMO organisation chart.
[161] These roles are flexible and can change to suit your requirements.

Figure 13: Typical hierarchy structure of PMO (Unito)

Services provided by PMO

The Project Management Office will undertake the following services: [161]
[162] [163]

- strategic planning and making the governance of the project. This responsibility will include selecting the projects to undertake that align with the organisation's goals and the criteria defining the project
- select the most appropriate project management methodology for each project. Identifying gaps that may occur in the methodologies of project management
- develop best practices in standards and workflow processes that align with the organisation's goals, ensuring best practices are standardised but flexible enough when there are changes to projects
- to control the project
- to promote the management of each project

- developing and maintaining a project culture
- training the project management leaders and team members
- allocation of resources to each project
- communicate to other team members and all employees across the organisation.

Benefits of a PMO

A PMO can provide the following benefits [161] to your organisation:

- the PMO will align projects with the organisation's strategies and goals
- improve communication across the organisation
- ensure that projects are kept on track
- better control to ensure that projects are delivered under or on budget
- the PMO team will become specifically skilled as they become more experienced with the management of projects.

12.5. What is the difference between PMO and CMO?

First, let's look at the common features between a Change Management Office (CMO) and Project Management Office (PMO). There are many commonalities, but the three common types are shown in Figure 16.

The main commonalities between CMO and PMO are that both ensure best practices and alignment with an organisation's goals.

Other commonalities include (i) they both exist to drive efficiencies, (ii) to increase adoption, (iii) to promote trust and (iv) to provide consistency and stability.[164]

Understanding the differences between a CMO and PMO will allow you to determine the best structure for your organisation. Reference is made to Table 23, which provides the differences between CMO and PMO.

CHANGE MANAGEMENT OFFICE (CMO)	PROJECT MANAGEMENT OFFICE (PMO)
The change is typically applied across the entire organisation but can be specific to a project	The change is applied to a project. The project can be applied across the organisation or can be specific to a department
The team will be experienced across all segments of change management	The team will be experienced in project management. The experience may not be organisation specific
A CMO can be found in any type of organisation across all industry sectors	A PMO is likely to be found in project-based organisations only
A successful CMO blends with the organisation's culture	A PMO may not blend into the organisation's culture

Table 23: Differences between Change Management Office and Project Management Office

12.6. Benefits of lessons learned

The failure rate of transformational change

What is the success rate for managing change within your organisation? Have you managed a success rate of 100% in driving change in your organisation? The chances are that the answer will be NO. If you have achieved a 100% success rate for change management, congratulations: it has been reported that transformational change has resulted in a failure rate of 70% – and that failure rate was before the COVID-19 pandemic [165]. It is not surprising that this failure rate is high as most organisations do not frequently undergo transformational change. Transformational change may occur occasionally or rarely; hence the failure rate will likely be high as the organisation is unprepared for change. For an organisation that undergoes transformational change many times, its success rate will be high as it will have learned from previous failures.[166]

The key reasons for such a high failure rate [165] are because:

- transformational change is not part of the organisation's primary activities
- organisations do not have the disciplines in place to manage potential risks
- organisations do not have the skilled or experienced employees to manage the change
- organisations do not measure the outcome or progress throughout each stage of the change
- the organisation's goals have changed, and the change management is not aligned with the new goals.

Transformation life cycle

Understanding and coming to grips with the key areas where failure can occur throughout the transformation life cycle will make you aware of areas where you can prepare preventative strategies to minimise risk in your organisation. The transformation life cycle consists of four elements (i) target setting, (ii) planning, (iii) implementation and (iv) after implementation. According to McKinsey & Company, their survey results [166] showed the percentage failure rates at the following stages of the transformation life cycle:

Failure Points

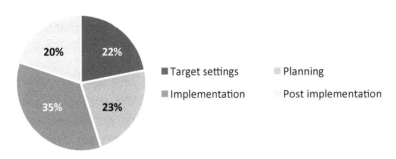

Figure 14: Failure points in the transformation life cycle

Therefore, at each stage of the transformational life cycle, an organisation must apply transformation disciplines.

Your organisation does not have to be large to consider transformation disciplines. The transformation disciplines that should be implemented include greater communication, frequent meetings, frequent tracking of progress, performance reviews at all levels and allocation of capital, talent and IT resources.

Learning from the past

> **"It's fine to celebrate success, but it is more important to heed the lessons of failure."**
>
> *Bill Gates*

The learning lesson should have a measurable impact (good or bad) [167] and must focus on answering three questions (i) what happened, (ii) why it happened and (iii) how it happened. The learning lesson must be valid (factually correct) and appropriate to provide a solution that can be used in future changes.

Failures should not be considered a lost cause. A transformational change that did not succeed may not be a complete failure. There may be some great success stories within the transformation process that should be heeded for future transformational changes.

Although it is important to learn the lessons of what went right (success) and what did not go right (failure), an organisation should not just limit itself to learning about past failures. The success lessons can easily be implemented into future transformational change, but similarly, the lessons learned from failures can be used to change the processes and activities for future changes. The learning lessons are known as agile retrospectives because the lesson is about the past performance of activities and processes.[168] However, these agile retrospective learnings are valuable when (a) learning about the past and (b) putting them to use in future changes.

The differences between lessons learned and retrospectives [169] are summarised in Table 24.

	LESSONS LEARNED	RETROSPECTIVES
Definition	Positive and negative knowledge learnt from the project or change	Inspect the team involved with the change and development of an improvement plan
Reality	Typically takes place at the end of the project. Ideally, the lessons learned should be undertaken throughout the project (at each milestone)	Fixed to a timebox mindset. It looks at the requirements, design, planning, reviews and deployment

Positives	Positives gained can be used for future change	Positive learnings are based on whether the team worked effectively during the timebox
Negatives	Negatives learned are typically shifted to the person or team for blame	Negative learnings are used to develop the "form, storm, norm and perform" mentality

Table 24: Differences between lessons learned and retrospectives

There are two types of retrospectives – (i) project retrospectives and (ii) release retrospectives.

The types of projects are non-recurring (mergers, acquisitions, new IT resources etc.). Project retrospectives typically occur at the end of a project. Enhancing the project retrospective learning would be best at all stages (milestones) of the project, not just at the end, as lessons learned after each milestone can be applied to the remaining milestones that need to be completed [170].

Release retrospectives are predominantly used to release a new product or service. The lessons learned from this retrospective are more complex as it looks at the people involved across the organisation. It takes longer to determine the success and failure factors.

When learning goes wrong!

There are always good intentions to implement the lessons learned from the past and incorporate these lessons into future transformational change. However, it is not always a smooth pathway when the lessons learned still go wrong. Let's take a moment to understand why learning does go wrong:[171]

- the employees are treated as human resources and not as human beings
- the team do not celebrate when they have achieved a milestone or completed the change
- the organisation only focuses on what went wrong rather than the whole change (the good and bad parts)
- the time ratio is not realistic and does not fit the change
- when the lesson's goal is to find people who will act as a scapegoat for the failure
- the team that was part of the change has been disbanded.

Chapter Summary

This chapter has presented the idea of setting up a Change Management Office (CMO) or Project Management Office (PMO) that you can use for your next change or project. The CMO is more flexible and can be used across all industry sectors and any sized organisation. PMOs are predominantly used for project orientated organisations but can be used effectively for your next transformational change.

Remember that each change managed throughout your organisation needs to be (i) measured and (ii) to learn the lessons throughout the change. Both measurement and lessons to be learned must take place after completing each milestone, not just at the end of the change. The measurement of key metrics will help determine the reasons for success or failure.

Lessons to be learned should also be performed throughout every stage of the change.

Finally, a lesson should be undertaken on each successful and failed milestone so they can be applied to future changes undertaken by your organisation.

13. Tips to successfully sustain change in your organisation

The transformation change must last for an extended period and not be considered an episodic change (a short-term change similar to completing a project). There is no point in undergoing organisational change if the change is short-lived. Your organisational change must be sustainable for the long-term period. The change in your organisation took time and effort and most likely incurred a cost. Therefore the change is an investment, and you want to get a return on your investment sometime in the future.

Even though it is mentioned that your transformational change must be sustainable, the change cannot be rigid. The change must be flexible enough when the internal, market and economic conditions change.

This chapter outlines the importance of making your change sustainable and guides you in ensuring that the transformation change remains workable after completion.

13.1. Importance of making your transformation change sustainable

Problems with sustainable change

PROBLEM ONE. Too often, organisations will make a new change based on what they think their customers want. The organisations make these changes based on their reputation rather than working with the customer. For example, major smartphone providers constantly introduce new phones or update existing phones with new features. Some of these new phones will flop in the marketplace, whilst others will become a hit. The point raised here is that there is no sustainable change happening within the organisation as the variables are constantly changing. To resolve this type of problem, an organisation needs to listen and react to the market. But the culture of the organisation needs to be positioned to be a change-oriented culture.

PROBLEM TWO. Organisations do not necessarily have the best-fit employees with experience in change management. Hiring change employees will help transform the culture to become more oriented toward change.

PROBLEM THREE. Organisations find that making a change can be difficult and often complex. These organisations fail to ensure that the change is sustainable through a lack of planning and future strategic direction.

Embodying change in the organisation

There are no hard-and-fast rules for embodying change in an organisation. There are few precedents that organisations can follow as change does not become public knowledge. Once transformation change is incorporated into an organisation, future changes become more straightforward as it becomes the usual way of conducting business with stakeholders. Sustainable change moves from the old concept of making a determined effort to change, where resistance can become a barrier to change, to a more acceptable effort to change.[172] The acceptable effort to change must flow through to every person in the organisation, and this can only occur by utilising behavioural change management.

The organisation's culture needs to be critically assessed to see if it fits with the changing environment.[173] Organisations have a dominant culture, but underneath this dominant culture lies sub-cultures. The sub-cultures may not necessarily align with the dominant culture.

13.2. Applying sustainable changes to your organisation

There are multiples of various ideas presented by respected organisations, leaders and authors on how to make the change in your organisation sustainable for the future.

Katelyn Bair: five pillars to making your change sustainable

Katelyn Bair, founder and marketing manager at Plansight Marketing, LLC, points out that an organisation can adopt five pillars to make its change sustainable.[174] I have listed these in Table 25.

1ST PILLAR	2ND PILLAR	3RD PILLAR	4TH PILLAR	5TH PILLAR
Leadership	Strategy	Culture	Structure	Systems
Sustainable change starts from the top of the company – the leaders The leaders must have a strong vision and motivate the employees to move toward the vision	The strategies must support the organisation's vision If the strategies are strong and effective, the strategies can become embedded into the organisation's culture	The people, the core beliefs and environments will formulate the organisation's culture The vision and strategies should be embedded into the culture	The organisation needs to examine how to align change strategies with the existing capabilities and limitations of the present structures	Systems determine how the organisation operates. If the existing systems work well, then the organisation will function efficiently, and transformational change will have a greater chance of success

Table 25: Five Pillars for Sustainable Change

Don Tennant: tips for driving change

Respected author of IT Business, Don Tennant, has compiled a list of changes that can be used in your organisation. These tips were sourced from professional development coaches Christina Tangora Schlachter and Terry H. Hildebrandt (both recognised as professional development coaches) in their book named "Leading Business Change for Dummies." They believe that organisations should adopt the following tips [175] to drive sustainable change:

As a leader and manager, you must believe in the change yourself. Express your belief in the change to other people in the organisation and align your priorities with the organisation's goals.

You must be at the forefront of change: an early adopter.

Change your attitude, behaviours, and beliefs.

Be there to influence others; you can't change yourself.

Be prepared to back up the change with proven data and demonstrate the benefits to other people.

Be at the forefront of communication with your people. Encourage your people to be communicative.

As a leader and manager, it is your responsibility to help other people to be able to manage the change.

Model for sustainable change

Respected CEO of Harrington Associates, Dr H. James Harrington, compiled a Sustainable Change White Paper in conjunction with Frank Voehl and Christopher F. Voehl, CEO and CIO of Strategy Associates, respectively. [176] The authors' sustainable model consisted of seven components:

1. There must be evidence that the change is supported by the top leaders and managers of the organisation.
2. Assess the readiness for change before the change is implemented. Allow for flexibility before, during and post-implementation of the change.
3. The approaches taken to managing the change must be sustainable even after the change has been implemented.
4. There must be ongoing communication between the management and the employees before, during, and after implementing the change.
5. The change will never be constant. Changes will continually occur in the future, and the paradigms must shift and be flexible enough to handle change.
6. Consider the use of change agents to ensure that the change is sustained.
7. Invest in the right people, new capacities, new technologies and innovations. Investment into these areas will enable change to become sustainable.

Martin Orridge, the respected author of the book named "Change Leadership, developing a Change-Adept Organization", identifies that change can be difficult to accomplish when the change involves humans. [177] An organisation will be successful with sustainable change if leaders and managers assist employees in coping with the change. Chapter 3 of his book outlines 75 ideas on transformation techniques for sustaining change within any organisation. From those ideas, I have selected what I believe to be the twenty most important techniques that you should consider adopting.[177]

1. Embrace change as an opportunity for the present and the future.
2. Be driven by change as it keeps your organisation a step ahead of your competitors.
3. Change should be seen as being essential.
4. There must be benefits arising from the change, and these benefits must be sustainable.
5. Leaders and managers must be committed to the change. Their commitment must be seen by employees.
6. Leaders and management should be at the forefront of the change with strong leadership.
7. Develop a need for urgency through ambition with the change and pass this urgency down to all employees.
8. Ensure that the organisation's goals are SMART and achievable.
9. Regularly review and change the Strategic Management Plan and Processes.
10. Communicate the organisation's vision to employees to participate in the continual achievement of the vision.
11. Communication between leaders, managers and employees is paramount before, during and after the change.
12. Allow employees to consider the concept of the change and how it will impact them.
13. Encourage employees and empower them to make decisions about the change.
14. Respect the employees for their level of professionalism.
15. Create a culture that fosters openness within the organisation.

16. Encourage the transfer of knowledge and skills between employees.
17. Develop a philosophy of continuous learning for your employees by establishing a learning plan to be applied across the organisation.
18. Develop the tools and resources that will assist with and complement the future change effectively and efficiently.
19. Develop a strong and flexible risk management plan.
20. Reward employees for successful implementation of change.

Martin's valued listing of transformational techniques is shaped around making a sustainable change in your organisation.

Chapter Summary

A change must benefit the organisation, its people, and stakeholders (shareholders, customers, and suppliers). The desired benefits can be financial, operational, innovative or strategically beneficial to the stakeholders.

The change in any organisation can be sustainable, providing that every person is involved and agrees with the change. If leaders, managers and employees are aligned with the change, the change will be successful. This chapter has provided valuable tips on making your next change sustainable for the long term.

A note from the author...

Using our rich change and project management methodologies and experience, the Delph Solutions team helps executives, teams, and organisations overcome challenges to achieve their goals.

Our unique, proven methods have delivered outstanding results and set us apart from other consulting firms because we take a personal approach: we put the people at the heart of all we do. Our clients gain confidence, increase their capabilities and are empowered to become better leaders.

We can support and manage large international organisations' change programmes, so if you require support for your business or personal transformation, we would be delighted to hear from you. You can find more information on www.delphsolutions.com and www.yvonnedeville.com.

Yvonne

References

[1] Tutor2U, "Causes and Types of Change," n.d.. [Online]. Available: https://www.tutor2u.net/business/reference/causes-and-types-of-change.

[2] Capgemini, "Behavioural Change Management in the Virtual World," 8 November 2013. [Online]. Available: https://www.capgemini.com/gb-en/2013/11/behavioural-change-management-in-the-virtual-world/.

[3] MTD Training, "The Three Types Of Change," 21 April 2009. [Online]. Available: https://www.mtdtraining.com/blog/three-types-of-change.htm.

[4] Othering & Belonging Institute, "Transactional versus Transformative Change," n.d.. [Online]. Available: https://belonging.berkeley.edu/transactional-versus-transformative-change.

[5] D. Brandenberg, "What Problems Do Employees Create When They Resist Change in the Workplace?," n.d.. [Online]. Available: https://smallbusiness.chron.com/problems-employees-create-resist-change-workplace-15826.html.

[6]   Kaizen Consulting Group, "Negative Effects of Resistance to
        Change," n.d.. [Online]. Available: https://www.kcg.com.sg/
        negative-effects-of-resistance-to-change/.

[7]   CMS Wire, "Why Human Behavior Is Key to Successful Change
        Management," 10 July 2019. [Online]. Available: https://www.
        cmswire.com/digital-workplace/why-human-behavior-is-key-to-
        successful-change-management/.

[8]   Prosci, "The History and Future of Change Management," n.d..
        [Online]. Available: https://www.prosci.com/resources/articles/
        change-management-history-and-future.

[9]   K. Cherry, "Maslow's Hierarchy of Needs," 14 February 2022.
        [Online]. Available: https://www.verywellmind.com/what-is-
        maslows-hierarchy-of-needs-4136760#:~:text=Abraham%20
        Maslow's%20hierarchy%20of%20needs,complex%20needs%20
        at%20the%20top..

[10]   D. S. McLeod, "Maslow's Hierarchy of Needs," 29 December 2020.
        [Online]. Available: https://www.simplypsychology.org/maslow.
        html.

[11]   London School of Hygiene & Tropical Medicine, "Module 1:
        Behaviour Change Theory – Outline," n.d.. [Online]. Available:
        https://www.lshtm.ac.uk/media/11191.

[12]   Deepsense, "What is reinforcement learning? The complete
        guide," 5 July 2018. [Online]. Available: https://deepsense.ai/what-
        is-reinforcement-learning-the-complete-guide/.

[13]   A. Poddiachyi, "Reinforcement Learning, Brain, and Psychology:
        Introduction," 21 November 2019. [Online]. Available: https://
        towardsdatascience.com/reinforcement-learning-brain-and-
        psychology-part-1-introduction-b5f79a0475ab.

[14] Minnesota Pollution Control Agency, "The Psychology of Sustainable Behavior," September 2009. [Online]. Available: https://www.pca.state.mn.us/sites/default/files/p-ee1-01.pdf.

[15] A. Baggio, E. Digentiki and R. Varma, "Organizations do not change. People change!," 7 October 2019. [Online]. Available: https://www.mckinsey.com/business-functions/people-and-organizational-performance/our-insights/the-organization-blog/organizations-do-not-change-people-change.

[16] IDBS, "The Most Important Factor in Change Management? People.," 6 November 2013. [Online]. Available: https://www.idbs.com/2013/11/the-most-important-factor-in-change-management-people/.

[17] R. Dilts, "What Is NLP?," 2016. [Online]. Available: http://nlpu.com/NLPU_WhatIsNLP.html.

[18] Hypnosis and NLP, "The 13 Presuppositions of the NLP," 1 March 2013. [Online]. Available: http://www.hypnosisandnlp.co.uk/nlp/the-13-presuppositions-of-the-nlp.

[19] T. Dotz, "MAJOR PRESUPPOSITIONS OF NLP: The Top 13 Original Major Presuppositions of NLP Defined," n.d.. [Online]. Available: https://nlpco.com/presuppositions-of-nlp/.

[20] NLP Sure, "13 NLP presuppositions- the best guide you will need with NLP presuppositions exercise," n.d.. [Online]. Available: https://nlpsure.com/13-nlp-presuppositions/.

[21] Your Strategic Marketing Partner, "WHAT IS KOTTER'S 8 STEP CHANGE MODEL? (EXPLAINED)," n.d.. [Online]. Available: https://strategicmarketingpartner.com/what-is-kotters-8-step-change-model/.

[22] Staff, Masterclass, "How to Negotiate: The 5 Stages of the Negotiation Process," 8 November 2020. [Online]. Available:

https://www.masterclass.com/articles/how-to-negotiate#what-is-negotiation.

[23] R. L. Englund, "Executive Consultant, Englund Project Management Consultancy," 2010.

[24] G. Subramanian, "What is BATNA? How to Find Your Best Alternative to a Negotiated Agreement," 2 December 2021. [Online]. Available: https://www.pon.harvard.edu/daily/batna/translate-your-batna-to-the-current-deal/.

[25] Harvard Law School, "What is a BATNA?," n.d.. [Online]. Available: https://www.pon.harvard.edu/tag/batna/.

[26] Staff, Masterclass, "7 Negotiation Principles From Former Hostage Negotiator Chris Voss," 16 June 2021. [Online]. Available: https://www.masterclass.com/articles/negotiation-principles-from-former-hostage-negotiator-chris-voss#who-is-chris-voss.

[27] A. Hayes, "Undue Influence," 30 March 2021. [Online]. Available: https://www.investopedia.com/terms/u/undue-influence.asp.

[28] Workopolis, "8 difficult office personalities and how to work with them," 5 September 2017. [Online]. Available: https://careers.workopolis.com/advice/8-difficult-office-personalities-and-how-to-work-with-them/.

[29] Change Factory, "Managing Change: Dealing with the difficult people," n.d.. [Online]. Available: https://www.changefactory.com.au/our-thinking/articles/managing-change-dealing-difficult-people/.

[30] Freshbooks, "How to Deal with Difficult Employees: 10 Tips to Improve Workplace Performance," n.d.. [Online]. Available: https://www.freshbooks.com/hub/leadership/deal-with-difficult-employees.

[31] D. Codella, "How to Improve the Change Management Process for 7 Key Personality Types," 12 June 2018. [Online]. Available: https://www.wrike.com/blog/change-management-process-for-7-key-personality-types/.

[32] G. Wyles, "The eight personalities involved in change management programmes," 27 December 2013. [Online]. Available: https://www.hrzone.com/lead/change/the-eight-personalities-involved-in-change-management-programmes.

[33] D. Garvin and M. Roberto, "Change Through Persuasion," February 2005. [Online]. Available: https://hbr.org/2005/02/change-through-persuasion.

[34] Lead Change, "The Power of Persuasion," 12 January 2011. [Online]. Available: https://leadchangegroup.com/the-power-of-persuasion/.

[35] M. Toledo, "Business Tools: The Art Of Listening," 30 May 2018. [Online]. Available: https://www.forbes.com/sites/forbeslacouncil/2018/05/30/business-tools-the-art-of-listening/?sh=241c6eab26b1.

[36] D. Barnard, "Active Listening Skills, Examples and Exercises," 20 September 2017. [Online]. Available: https://virtualspeech.com/blog/active-listening-skills-examples-and-exercises.

[37] English Club, "What is Listening?," n.d.. [Online]. Available: https://www.englishclub.com/listening/what.htm.

[38] IN PD, "Six important benefits of active listening in the workplace," n.d.. [Online]. Available: https://inpd.co.uk/blog/benefits-of-active-listening/.

[39] Master Class, "How to Use Active Listening to Improve Your Communication Skills," 2 November 2021. [Online]. Available: https://www.masterclass.com/articles/how-to-use-active-listening-to-improve-your-communication-skills.

[40] C. Moore, "Lessons in Change Management: Deep Listening is Essential," 11 July 2019. [Online]. Available: https://teamheller. com/resources/blog/lessons-in-change-management-deep-listening-is-essential.

[41] Fabrik Brands, "Body language in business: Decoding the signals," n.d.. [Online]. Available: https://fabrikbrands. com/body-language-in-business/#:~:text=Business%20relationships%20are%20 built%20on%20communication.&text=Body%20language%20 in%20business%20sets,the%20largest%20volumes%20of%20 information..

[42] GCF Global, "The power of body language," n.d.. [Online]. Available: https://edu.gcfglobal.org/en/business-communication/ the-power-of-body-language/1/.

[43] The University of Texas, "How Much of Communication Is Nonverbal?," n.d.. [Online]. Available: https://online.utpb.edu/ about-us/articles/communication/how-much-of-communication-is-nonverbal/.

[44] CIPHR, "10 persuasion techniques to help you get ahead at work," n.d.. [Online]. Available: https://www.ciphr.com/advice/10-persuasion-techniques-to-use-at-work/.

[45] Cherry, K., "Utilizing Emotional Intelligence in the Workplace," 2020. [Online]. Available: https://www.verywellmind.com/utilizing-emotional-intelligence-in-the-workplace-4164713.

[46] TSW Training, "Daniel Goleman's Emotional Intelligence in Leadership: How to improve motivation," 14 October 2021. [Online]. Available: https://www.tsw.co.uk/blog/leadership-and-management/daniel-goleman-emotional-intelligence/.

[47] C. Cassata, "The Benefits of Emotional Intelligence (EQ) at Work," 27 September 2021. [Online]. Available: https://psychcentral.com/ blog/the-benefits-of-emotional-intelligence#eq-definition.

[48] DifferenceBetween.com, "Difference Between Logic and Reason," 8 November 2016. [Online]. Available: https://www.differencebetween.com/difference-between-logic-and-vs-reason/.

[49] Centre for Practical Wisdom, "The Wise Mind: How logical reasoning can help manage emotions," 4 June 2020. [Online]. Available: https://wisdomcenter.uchicago.edu/news/discussions/wise-mind-how-logical-reasoning-can-help-manage-emotions.

[50] Cambridge Dictionary, "Credibility," n.d.. [Online]. Available: https://dictionary.cambridge.org/dictionary/english/credibility.

[51] M. Lemonis, "What is Credibility in Business?," n.d.. [Online]. Available: https://www.marcuslemonis.com/business/credibility-in-business.

[52] Klemchuk LLP, "The Importance of Honesty in the Workplace," 31 January 2014. [Online]. Available: https://www.klemchuk.com/ideate/importance-of-honesty-in-workplace.

[53] K. Cherry, "What Is Motivation?," 27 April 2020. [Online]. Available: https://www.verywellmind.com/what-is-motivation-2795378.

[54] Success4, "9 TYPES OF MOTIVATION THAT MAKE IT POSSIBLE TO REACH YOUR DREAMS," n.d.. [Online]. Available: https://success4.com/blog/9-types-of-motivation-that-make-it-possible-to-reach-your-dreams/.

[55] Cherry, K., "What Motivation Theory Can Tell Us About Human Behavior," 17 April 2021. [Online]. Available: https://www.verywellmind.com/theories-of-motivation-2795720.

[56] UK Essays, "Theories of Motivation in Business Management," 18 June 2018. [Online]. Available: https://www.ukessays.com/essays/business/motivation-in-the-modern-business-world-business-essay.php.

[57]   Mind Tools, "SMART Goals," n.d.. [Online]. Available: https://www.
mindtools.com/pages/article/smart-goals.htm.

[58]   K. Cherry, "What Is Self-Concept?," 18 April 2021. [Online].
Available: https://www.verywellmind.com/what-is-self-
concept-2795865.

[59]   Open Sourced Workplace, "52 Employee Engagement KPI's," n.d..
[Online]. Available: https://opensourcedworkplace.com/news/52-
employee-engagement-kpi-s.

[60]   Thomson Reuters, "20 ways employees at Thomson Reuters
are motivated by their work," n.d.. [Online]. Available: https://
www.thomsonreuters.com/en/careers/careers-blog/20-ways-
employees-are-motivated-by-work.html.

[61]   T. Powell, "Strategy as Diligence: Putting Behavioral Strategy into
Practice," Sage Journals, pp. 162-190, 2017.

[62]   A. Hamilton, "Social Motivation," 15 September 2017. [Online].
Available: http://serious-science.org/social-motivation-8756.

[63]   S. Mcleod, "Social Influence," 2021. [Online]. Available: https://
www.simplypsychology.org/a-level-social.html.

[64]   Cherry, K., "An Overview of the Myers-Briggs Type Indicator," 23
July 2021. [Online]. Available: https://www.verywellmind.com/the-
myers-briggs-type-indicator-2795583.

[65]   H. Priebe, "How To Motivate Each Myers-Briggs Personality Type,"
13 October 2015. [Online]. Available: https://thoughtcatalog.
com/heidi-priebe/2015/10/how-to-motivate-each-myers-briggs-
personality-type/.

[66]   Managementhelp.org, "What is an Organization?," n.d.. [Online].
Available: https://managementhelp.org/organizations/definition.
htm.

[67] Business Jargon, "Organization," n.d.. [Online]. Available: https://businessjargons.com/organization.html.

[68] Managementhelp.org, "What Makes Each Organization Unique," n.d.. [Online]. Available: https://managementhelp.org/organizations/unique.htm.

[69] MindTools, "Managing in a VUCA World," 2020. [Online]. Available: https://www.mindtools.com/pages/article/managing-vuca-world.htm#:~:text=VUCA%20stands%20for%20volatility%2C%20uncertainty,day%2Dto%2Dday%20working..

[70] N. Bennett and G. Lemoine, "What VUCA Really Means for You," January – February 2014. [Online]. Available: https://hbr.org/2014/01/what-vuca-really-means-for-you.

[71] H. Harper, "The Stages of Group Formation, and how they Aid Your Teams Success," 29 March 2019. [Online]. Available: https://www.workstyle.io/stages-of-team-development.

[72] Your Article Library, "4 Important Theories of Group Formation (With Diagram)," n.d.. [Online]. Available: https://www.yourarticlelibrary.com/organization/group-dynamics/4-important-theories-of-group-formation-with-diagram/63900.

[73] A. Puscasu, "8 Best Team Building Methods Series – Homan and Tuckman Methods," 16 September 2021. [Online]. Available: http://apepm.co.uk/the-8-best-team-building-methods-homan-and-tuckman/.

[74] UK Essays, "Importance of groups to organizations and individuals," 16 May 2017. [Online]. Available: https://www.ukessays.com/essays/management/importance-of-groups-to-organizations-and-individuals-management-essay.php.

[75] Your Article Library, "Groups Found in an Organisation (4 Types)," n.d.. [Online]. Available: https://www.yourarticlelibrary.com/organization/groups-found-in-an-organisation-4-types/44999.

[76] Team Asana, "Group vs. team: What's the difference?," 14 October 2021. [Online]. Available: https://asana.com/resources/group-vs-team.

[77] Agile Alliance, "Team," n.d.. [Online]. Available: https://www.agilealliance.org/glossary/team/#q=~(infinite~false~filters~(postType~(~'page~'post~'aa_book~'aa_event_session~'aa_experience_report~'aa_glossary~'aa_research_paper~'aa_video)~ tags ~(~'team))~searchTerm~'~sort~false~sortDirection~'asc~page~1).

[78] J. Smart, "How to use the 5 stages of team development (and build better teams!)," 11 February 2021. [Online]. Available: https://www.sessionlab.com/blog/team-development/.

[79] M. Kojic, "The 5 stages of group development explained," 22 December 2021. [Online]. Available: https://clockify.me/blog/business/stages-of-group-development/.

[80] University of Birmingham, "Tips for Effective Group Working," n.d.. [Online]. Available: https://www.birmingham.ac.uk/schools/metallurgy-materials/about/cases/group-work/tips.aspx#:~:text=Discuss%20how%20you%20are%20going,them%20to%20individuals%20or%20subgroups..

[81] Peeps HR, "OUR TOP 10 TIPS FOR EFFECTIVE TEAMWORK," n.d.. [Online]. Available: https://www.peepshr.co.uk/resource-centre/our-top-10-tips-for-effective-teamwork/.

[82] R. Conley, "6 Strategies for Helping Your Team Manage Change," 14 September 2014. [Online]. Available: https://leadingwithtrust.com/2014/09/14/6-strategies-for-helping-your-team-manage-change/.

[83] Kadabra, "6 Barriers to Organizational Change and How to Overcome Them," 28 August 2018. [Online]. Available: https://www.wearekadabra.com/2018/08/28/6-barriers-to-organizational-change-and-how-to-overcome-them/.

[84] Prosci, "AVOID THESE 5 CHANGE MANAGEMENT OBSTACLES," n.d.. [Online]. Available: https://blog.prosci.com/avoid-these-change-management-obstacles.

[85] Forbes, "https://www.forbes.com/sites/williamcraig/2018/09/05/the-role-leadership-has-in-company-culture/?sh=4197bd2e16b6#:~:text=The%20Role%20Leadership%20Has%20In%20Company%20Culture," 5 September 2018. [Online]. Available: https://www.forbes.com/sites/williamcraig/2018/09/05/the-role-leadership-has-in-company-culture/?sh=4197bd2e16b6.

[86] AlignOrg Solutions, "The Role of Leadership in Change Management," 9 February 2021. [Online]. Available: https://alignorg.com/the-role-of-leadership-in-change-management/.

[87] Forbes, "New Study Explores Why Change Management Fails – And How To (Perhaps) Succeed," 4 September 2013. [Online]. Available: https://www.forbes.com/sites/victorlipman/2013/09/04/new-study-explores-why-change-management-fails-and-how-to-perhaps-succeed/?sh=3d2672ea7137.

[88] Bizfluent, "Negative Effects of Change Management," 10 December 2018. [Online]. Available: https://bizfluent.com/info-8533922-negative-effects-change-management.html.

[89] Expert Program Management, "Leadership Styles," February 2017. [Online]. Available: https://expertprogrammanagement.com/2017/02/leadership-styles/.

[90] Hubspot, "The 8 Most Common Leadership Styles & How to Find Your Own [Quiz]," n.d.. [Online]. Available: https://blog.hubspot.com/marketing/leadership-styles.

[91] Corpbiz, "Importance of Corporate Governance in an Organization," 2 April 2020. [Online]. Available: https://corpbiz.io/learning/importance-of-corporate-governance-in-an-organization/.

[92] S. Bell, "You need effective leadership for good governance," 25 June 2019. [Online]. Available: https://www.grantthornton.co.uk/insights/five-principles-of-good-governance--leadership/.

[93] D. L. Ackerman, "Creating Effective Change Governance for Your Change Initiative: Who's in Charge of What?," 19 December 2016. [Online]. Available: https://blog.beingfirst.com/creating-effective-change-governance-for-your-change-initiative-whos-in-charge-of-what.

[94] Value-Based Management, "Summary of the Six Change Approaches by Kotter (Abstract)," n.d.. [Online]. Available: https://www.valuebasedmanagement.net/methods_kotter_change_approaches.html.

[95] Prosci, "5 Tips for Managing Resistance to Change," n.d.. [Online]. Available: https://www.prosci.com/resources/articles/tips-for-managing-resistance-to-change.

[96] Expert Program Management, "Six Change Approaches," May 2018. [Online]. Available: https://expertprogrammanagement.com/2018/05/six-change-approaches/.

[97] BMC, "Lewin's 3 Stage Model of Change Explained," 5 November 2019. [Online]. Available: https://www.bmc.com/blogs/lewin-three-stage-model-change/.

[98] Airiodin, "What are the Advantages and Disadvantages of Kurt Lewin's Change Model? Everything You Need to Know, including Pros and Cons.," n.d.. [Online]. Available: https://www.airiodion.com/kurt-lewin-change-model/.

[99] MindTools, "Lewin's Change Management Model," n.d.. [Online]. Available: https://www.mindtools.com/pages/article/newPPM_94.htm.

[100]   Harvard Law School, "5 Conflict Resolution Strategies," 12 October 2021. [Online]. Available: https://www.pon.harvard.edu/daily/conflict-resolution/conflict-resolution-strategies/.

[101]   The Myer Briggs Company, "TKI® conflict resolution model," n.d.. [Online]. Available: https://eu.themyersbriggs.com/en/tools/TKI.

[102]   Kilmann Diagnostics, "AN OVERVIEW OF THE," n.d.. [Online]. Available: https://kilmanndiagnostics.com/overview-thomas-kilmann-conflict-mode-instrument-tki/#:~:text=The%20Thomas%2DKilmann%20Instrument%20is,people%20appear%20to%20be%20incompatible.&text=Competing%20is%20assertive%20and%20uncooperative,at%20the%20other%20person.

[103]   UC San Diego, "How to Handle Conflict in the Workplace," 5 January 2018. [Online]. Available: https://blink.ucsd.edu/HR/supervising/conflict/handle.html.

[104]   Prosci, "5 Tips for Managing Resistance to Change," n.d.. [Online]. Available: https://www.prosci.com/resources/articles/tips-for-managing-resistance-to-change.

[105]   ACCIPIO, "Preventing Conflict," n.d.. [Online]. Available: https://www.accipio.com/eleadership/mod/wiki/view.php?id=1884.

[106]   Accenture, "Outmanoeuvre uncertainty: What to do now and next," 11 May 2020. [Online]. Available: https://www.accenture.com/gb-en/about/company/coronavirus-business-economic-impact.

[107]   World Economic Forum, "From perfume to hand sanitiser, TVs to face masks: how companies are changing track to fight COVID-19," 24 March 2020. [Online]. Available: https://www.weforum.org/agenda/2020/03/from-perfume-to-hand-sanitiser-tvs-to-face-masks-how-companies-are-changing-track-to-fight-covid-19/.

[108] Forbes, "LVMH Converting Its Perfume Factories To Make Hand Sanitizer," 15 March 2020. [Online]. Available: https://www.forbes.com/sites/richardkestenbaum/2020/03/15/lvmh-converting-its-perfume-factories-to-make-hand-sanitizer/?sh=4f7e57b44a9a.

[109] BBC, "Coronavirus: iPhone manufacturer Foxconn to make masks," 7 February 2020. [Online]. Available: https://www.bbc.com/news/business-51410700.

[110] World Health Organization, "COVID-19 disrupting mental health services in most countries, WHO survey," 5 October 2020. [Online]. Available: https://www.who.int/news/item/05-10-2020-covid-19-disrupting-mental-health-services-in-most-countries-who-survey#:~:text=Bereavement%2C%20isolation%2C%20loss,outcomes%20and%20even%20death..

[111] United Nations, "COVID crisis to push global unemployment over 200 million mark in 2022," 2 June 2021. [Online]. Available: https://news.un.org/en/story/2021/06/1093182.

[112] AARP, "15 Lessons the Coronavirus Pandemic Has Taught Us," 4 March 2021. [Online]. Available: https://www.aarp.org/health/conditions-treatments/info-2021/lessons-from-covid.html.

[113] Accenture, "COVID-19: 5 new human truths that experiences need to address," 3 April 2020. [Online]. Available: https://www.accenture.com/gb-en/about/company/coronavirus-human-experience.

[114] Greater Good Magazine, "What We Learned About Human Behavior from the Pandemic," 7 July 2021. [Online]. Available: https://greatergood.berkeley.edu/article/item/what_we_learned_about_human_behavior_from_the_pandemic.

[115] E. Vyas, "What The Pandemic Has Taught Us About Change," 5 May 2021. [Online]. Available: https://www.forbes.com/sites/forbeshumanresourcescouncil/2021/05/05/what-the-pandemic-has-taught-us-about-change/?sh=20abd44c5239.

[116] CIPD, "What lessons can COVID-19 teach us about organisational change?," 12 June 2020. [Online]. Available: https://peopleprofession.cipd.org/insights/articles/lessons-covid-19-organisational-change#gref.

[117] World Economic Forum, "5 ways the COVID-19 pandemic is changing the role of leaders," 4 October 2021. [Online]. Available: https://www.weforum.org/agenda/2021/10/5-ways-the-pandemic-is-changing-the-role-of-leaders/.

[118] Omdia, "Future of Work – How Long-Term Digital Workplace Strategies and Business Priorities Have Changed," 2021. [Online]. Available: https://omdia.tech.informa.com/marketing/campaigns/future-of-work.

[119] Gartner, "9 Future of Work Trends Post-COVID-19," 29 April 2021. [Online]. Available: https://www.gartner.com/smarterwithgartner/9-future-of-work-trends-post-covid-19.

[120] People Management, "What has coronavirus taught us about leadership and where do we go from here?," 4 June 2020. [Online]. Available: https://www.peoplemanagement.co.uk/long-reads/articles/coronavirus-taught-leadership-where-go-from-here#gref.

[121] PwC, "Redefining a post-pandemic world," n.d.. [Online]. Available: https://www.pwc.com/mt/en/publications/humanresources/redefining-leadership-in-a-post-pandemic-world.html.

[122] IBM, "COVID-19 and the future of business," 2021. [Online]. Available: https://www.ibm.com/thought-leadership/institute-business-value/report/covid-19-future-business.

[123] Deloitte, "Confronting the crisis," 29 April 2020. [Online]. Available: https://www2.deloitte.com/us/en/insights/economy/covid-19/covid-19-crisis-management-in-financial-services.html?id=us:2em:3na:4di6738:5awa:6di:MMDDYY:&pkid=1007113.

[124] Factory Dev, "What is the role of digitalization in business growth?," n.d.. [Online]. Available: https://factory.dev/blog/digitalization-business-growth.

[125] The Enterprisers Project, "What is digital transformation?," n.d.. [Online]. Available: https://enterprisersproject.com/what-is-digital-transformation.

[126] V. Zhovtyuk, "Digital Transformation & Change Management: How to Be Ready," 7 August 2018. [Online]. Available: https://medium.com/@VitaliyZhovtyuk/digital-transformation-change-management-how-to-be-ready-8565b893243.

[127] Imaginovation, "What is Digital Transformation & Why It's Important for Businesses?," 1 December 2021. [Online]. Available: https://imaginovation.net/blog/what-is-digital-transformation-importance-for-businesses/#DT_strategy.

[128] IT Pro, "Five reasons why digital transformation is essential for business growth," 24 February 2021. [Online]. Available: https://www.itpro.co.uk/strategy/29899/three-reasons-why-digital-transformation-is-essential-for-business-growth#:~:text=Transformation%20can%20enable%20better%20collaboration,chance%20of%20thriving%20post%2Dpandemic..

[129] Gartner, "Gartner Identifies Six Key Steps to Build a Successful Digital Business," 21 May 2014. [Online]. Available: https://www.gartner.com/en/newsroom/press-releases/2014-05-21-gartner-identifies-six-key-steps-to-build-a-successful-digital-business.

[130] ZDNet, "Digital transformation is changing. Here's what comes next," 1 October 2021. [Online]. Available: https://www.zdnet.com/article/digital-transformation-is-changing-heres-what-comes-next/.

[131] Blue Car Technologies Limited, "Blue Car Technologies: 10 technology trends that will reshape businesses in 2022," 31 January 2022. [Online]. Available: https://www.

legalsupportnetwork.co.uk/resource/blue-car-technologies-10-technology-trends-that-will-reshape-businesses-in-2022/.

[132] [x]cube LABS, "10 Factors Defining Digital Transformation in 2022," 30 November 2021. [Online]. Available: https://www.xcubelabs.com/blog/10-factors-defining-digital-transformation-in-2022/.

[133] McKinsey, "Why industrials should pursue a tech-enabled transformation now," 7 November 2019. [Online]. Available: https://www.mckinsey.com/industries/advanced-electronics/our-insights/why-industrials-should-pursue-a-tech-enabled-transformation-now.

[134] McKinsey, "COVID-19: Implications for business," 2 February 2022. [Online]. Available: https://www.mckinsey.com/business-functions/risk-and-resilience/our-insights/covid-19-implications-for-business.

[135] Devpro Journal, "How Digital Transformation Strategies Will Change in 2022," 4 January 2022. [Online]. Available: https://www.devprojournal.com/technology-trends/digital-transformation/how-digital-transformation-strategies-will-change-in-2022/.

[136] World Economic Forum, "Predictions 2022: Business leaders on how can we ensure a safe and equitable digital transformation," 17 January 2022. [Online]. Available: https://www.weforum.org/agenda/2022/01/equitable-digital-transformation-business-leaders-davos-agenda-2022-digitization/.

[137] AI Multiple, "5 Digital Transformation Challenges in 2022," 27 January 2022. [Online]. Available: https://research.aimultiple.com/digital-transformation-challenges/.

[138] AI Multiple, "Top 7 Digital Transformation Best Practices for the Organizations," 10 January 2022. [Online]. Available: https://research.aimultiple.com/digital-transformation-best-practices/.

[139] K. Neher, "Twelve Digital Marketing Trends For 2022 And How To
       Take Advantage Of Them," 7 December 2021. [Online]. Available:
       https://www.forbes.com/sites/forbescoachescouncil/2021/12/07/
       twelve-digital-marketing-trends-for-2022-and-how-to-take-
       advantage-of-them/?sh=48cdf7187138.

[140] Rezaid, "How Artificial Intelligence is Changing the Future of
       Business," 15 July 2020. [Online]. Available: https://rezaid.co.uk/
       how-artificial-intelligence-is-changing-the-future-of-business/.

[141] Harvard Business Review, "Artificial Intelligence for the
       Real World," January 2018. [Online]. Available: https://hbr.
       org/2018/01/artificial-intelligence-for-the-real-world.

[142] IBM Cloud Education, "Artificial Intelligence (AI)," 3 June 2020.
       [Online]. Available: https://www.ibm.com/cloud/learn/what-is-
       artificial-intelligence.

[143] S. Russell and P. Norvig, "Artificial Intelligence: A Modern
       Approach," 2021. [Online]. Available: http://aima.cs.berkeley.edu/.

[144] CMSWire, "9 Ways AI Is Already Being Used in the Enterprise," 14
       April 2020. [Online]. Available: https://www.cmswire.com/digital-
       workplace/9-ways-ai-is-already-being-used-in-the-enterprise/.

[145] CMSWire, "6 Ways Artificial Intelligence Will Impact the Future
       Workplace," 17 April 2018. [Online]. Available: https://www.
       cmswire.com/information-management/6-ways-artificial-
       intelligence-will-impact-the-future-workplace/.

[146] D Labs, "How to implement Artificial Intelligence in your
       company?," 9 March 2020. [Online]. Available: https://dlabs.ai/
       blog/how-to-implement-ai-in-your-company/.

[147] Educba, "Introduction to Artificial Intelligence," n.d.. [Online].
       Available: https://www.educba.com/benefits-of-artificial-
       intelligence/.

[148] 10xDS, "Top 10 Benefits of Artificial Intelligence (AI)," 30 August 2020. [Online]. Available: https://10xds.com/blog/benefits-of-artificial-intelligence-ai/.

[149] Pew Research Center, "Artificial Intelligence and the Future of Humans," 18 December 2018. [Online]. Available: https://www.pewresearch.org/internet/2018/12/10/artificial-intelligence-and-the-future-of-humans/.

[150] The Conversation, "Worried about AI taking over the world? You may be making some rather unscientific assumptions," 24 September 2018. [Online]. Available: https://theconversation.com/worried-about-ai-taking-over-the-world-you-may-be-making-some-rather-unscientific-assumptions-103561.

[151] NCBI, "The impact of artificial intelligence on human society and bioethics," October 2020. [Online]. Available: https://www.ncbi.nlm.nih.gov/pmc/articles/PMC7605294/.

[152] Harvard Business Review, "Collaborative Intelligence: Humans and AI Are Joining Forces," July 2018. [Online]. Available: https://hbr.org/2018/07/collaborative-intelligence-humans-and-ai-are-joining-forces.

[153] S. Caredda, "Change Management: The 10 Best Approaches & Models," 14 April 2020. [Online]. Available: https://sergiocaredda.eu/organisation/change-management-the-10-best-approaches-models/.

[154] Prosci, "Metrics for Measuring Change Management," n.d.. [Online]. Available: https://www.prosci.com/resources/articles/measuring-change-management-effectiveness-with-metrics.

[155] C. Andrews, "Measuring the Success of Change Management," 5 September 2016. [Online]. Available: https://www.linkedin.com/pulse/measuring-success-change-management-collin-andrews-mba/.

[156] Project Manager, "5 Ways to Measure Project Success," 28 September 2015. [Online]. Available: https://www.projectmanager. com/blog/5-ways-to-measure-project-success.

[157] International Labour Organization, "BASIC PRINCIPLES OF MONITORING," n.d.. [Online]. Available: http://ilo.org/wcmsp5/ groups/public/---ed_emp/documents/publication/wcms_546505. pdf.

[158] M. Franklin, "Change Management Office – Benefits and Structure," August 2018. [Online]. Available: https:// agilechangemanagement.co.uk/wp-content/uploads/2018/08/ CMO-whitepaper-FINAL.pdf.

[159] Prosci, "The Change Management Office (CMO)," n.d.. [Online]. Available: https://www.prosci.com/resources/articles/change-management-office-primer.

[160] Issoria, "What is the value of a Change Management Office?," n.d.. [Online]. Available: https://issoriachange.com/articles/what-is-the-value-of-a-cmo.

[161] Unito, "What is PMO? A Guide to the Project Management Office," 24 November 2021. [Online]. Available: https://unito.io/ blog/what-is-pmo-project-management-office/#:~:text=Put%20 simply%2C%20a%20PMO%20is,project%20managers%20 within%20a%20company..

[162] Project Manager, "The Ultimate Guide to... Project Management Office (PMO)," n.d.. [Online]. Available: https://www. projectmanager.com/pmo.

[163] Project Engineer, "10 Roles and Responsibilities of a PMO," 15 February 2019. [Online]. Available: https://www.projectengineer. net/10-roles-and-responsibilities-of-a-pmo/.

[164] Loft9 Consulting, "Finding Stability in Change:," 2018. [Online]. Available: https://www.loft9consulting.com/wp-content/uploads/Loft9-Insights-Establishing-a-Change-Management-Office.pdf.

[165] Gotham Culture, "STOP GUESSING: HOW TO MEASURE THE IMPACT OF TRANSFORMATIONAL CHANGE," 20 July 2017. [Online]. Available: https://gothamculture.com/2017/07/20/measure-impact-transformational-change/.

[166] McKinsey & Company, "Losing from day one: Why even successful transformations fall short," 7 December 2021. [Online]. Available: https://www.mckinsey.com/business-functions/people-and-organizational-performance/our-insights/successful-transformations.

[167] Biztorming, "Incorporate Lessons Learned And Retrospectives To Improve Knowledge Sharing," 15 December 2020. [Online]. Available: https://biztorming.com/2020/12/15/incorporate-lessons-learned-and-retrospectives-to-improve-knowledge-sharing/.

[168] Atlassian Agile Coach, "Agile Retrospectives," n.d.. [Online]. Available: https://www.atlassian.com/agile/scrum/retrospectives.

[169] Association of Project Management, "Key differences between agile retrospectives and waterfall lessons learned," 5 August 2020. [Online]. Available: https://www.apm.org.uk/blog/key-differences-between-agile-retrospectives-and-waterfall-lessons-learned/.

[170] Helping Improve, "Why Project Retrospectives Are Challenging," n.d.. [Online]. Available: https://helpingimprove.com/why-project-retrospectives-are-challenging/.

[171] Helping Improve, "Lessons-Learned vs Project Retrospectives," n.d.. [Online]. Available: https://helpingimprove.com/lessons-learned-vs-project-retrospectives/.

[172] Simplicity HR, "Sustainable Change: Making It Happen," 7 December 2007. [Online]. Available: https://www.simplicityhr. com/hr-strategy/sustainable-change/#:~:text=When%20 achieved%2C%20sustainable%20change%20helps,on%20as%20 an%20academic%20dream.

[173] Ideas for Leaders, "ESTABLISHING SUSTAINABLE CHANGE IN ORGANIZATIONS," n.d.. [Online]. Available: https://www. ideasforleaders.com/ideas/establishing-sustainable-change-in-organizations.

[174] K. Bair, "Change Management Series – Part 5: Resistance to Change and the 5 Pillars," 2 June 2017. [Online]. Available: https://www. linkedin.com/pulse/change-management-series-part-5-resistance-pillars-katelyn-bair/.

[175] D. Tennant, "10 Tips for Driving Change in Your Organization from the Back Seat," 23 August 2012. [Online]. Available: https://www. itbusinessedge.com/it-management/10-tips-for-driving-change-in-your-organization-from-the-back-seat/.

[176] D. H. Harrington, F. Voehl and C. Voehl, "Model for Sustainable Change," 2015. [Online]. Available: https://www.pmi.org/learning/ library/model-sustainable-change-11122.

[177] M. Orridge, "Change Leadership, Developing a Change-Adept Organization," 2017. [Online]. Available: https://wellingtone. co.uk/75-ways-to-help-sustain-organisational-transformation/.

[178] Hubspot, "How to Win Friends and Influence People [Book Summary]," n.d.. [Online]. Available: https://www.hubspot.com/ sales/how-to-win-friends-and-influence-people-summary.

[179] Buchanan, Prof. D. and Huczynski, Dr A. Organizational Behaviour, 10th Edition, Pearson, 2020.

[180] A. Phillips, "How to Lead Your Team Through Change," 1 August 2014. [Online]. Available: https://www.entrepreneur.com/article/235832.

Images

List of Tables

List of Figures

About the author

Project and change management, goal setting and timely delivery have been in Yvonne's world from an early age. As a competitive figure ice-skater from the age of six, she needed to manage her time and training goals with schoolwork and competitions, unconsciously developing the skill of "project management".

A single mum at 18, Yvonne found ingenious solutions to practical obstacles in the often desperate challenges of juggling college/university, part-time work, and baby care alone, gaining further project management skills! After university, she became a consultant at PriceWaterhouseCoopers, gaining a solid understanding of corporate organisations.

Yvonne then (after redundancy) became an independent consultant, a role she has loved for over 20 years. She has supported and managed international programmes and business changes and transformations for organisations like Credit Suisse, Unilever/ekaterra, HSBC, Lloyds Banking Group, Barclays, Travelex, Clifford Chance, BP and Schroders.

Yvonne combines classic coaching styles and specialised behavioural psychology practices with various change and project management techniques. She has experience in structured and agile project management methodologies with certification in SAFe® 5 Agile, SCRUM, APMG, MSP, and PMP.

Her passion for knowledge and fascination for how the mind works led her to study more change and project management principles and methodologies: NLP, hypnosis, and various neurological re-patterning techniques. She became an NLP Master, Results Coach, and ILM Accredited Coach and obtained an Advanced Certificate in Neurological Repatterning and Performance Coaching. She has been working as an independent Results/Transformation Coach/ Mentor for over ten years.

Alongside her professional career, Yvonne served as a volunteer for the Youth-At-Risk UK Charity, helping Metropolitan University students within the Student Leadership Community Project: supporting them to achieve educational and personal goals and complete their programme of work. She is currently providing mentoring services to the Women in Technology network.

And if you're wondering if Yvonne continued to skate...
you'll have to ask her!

9 781739 642105